David Crystal

Listen to Your Child

A Parent's Guide to Children's Language

Penguin Books

PENGUIN BOOKS

Published by the Penguin Group
Penguin Books Ltd, 80 Strand, London WC2R 0RL, England
Penguin Putnam Inc., 375 Hudson Street, New York, New York 10014, USA
Penguin Books Australia Ltd, 250 Camberwell Road, Camberwell, Victoria 3124, Australia
Penguin Books Canada Ltd, 10 Alcorn Avenue, Toronto, Ontario, Canada M4V 3B2
Penguin Books India (P) Ltd, 11 Community Centre, Panchsheel Park, New Delhi – 110 017, India
Penguin Books (NZ) Ltd, Cnr Rosedale and Airborne Roads, Albany, Auckland, New Zealand
Penguin Books (South Africa) (Pty) Ltd, 24 Sturdee Avenue, Rosebank 2196, South Africa

Penguin Books Ltd, Registered Offices: 80 Strand, London WC2R 0RL, England

www.penguin.com

First published 1986
17

The cartoons on pp. 8, 36, 66, 112, 144, 212 and 222 are reproduced by kind permission of *Punch*. Those on p. 178 are reproduced by kind permission from *Children's Library* by Quentin Blake.

Printed in England by Clays Ltd, St Ives plc
Filmset in Monophoto Photina

ISBN-13: 978–0–14–011015–9

PENGUIN BOOKS

LISTEN TO YOUR CHILD

David Crystal was born in 1941 and spent the early years of his life in Holyhead, North Wales. He went to St Mary's College, Liverpool, and University College, London, where he read English and obtained his Ph.D. in 1966. He became lecturer in linguistics at University College, Bangor, and from 1965 to 1985 was at the University of Reading, where he was Professor of Linguistic Science for several years. He is currently Honorary Professor of Linguistics at the University of Wales, Bangor. His research interests are mainly in English language studies, and he has been much involved with the clinical and remedial applications of linguistics in the study of language handicap.

David Crystal has published numerous articles and reviews, and his books include *Linguistics* (Penguin 1971; second edition 1985), *Child Language Learning and Linguistics*, *Introduction to Language Pathology*, *A Dictionary of Linguistics and Phonetics*, *Clinical Linguistics*, *Profiling Linguistic Disability*, *Who Cares About English Usage?* (Penguin 1984; new edition 2000), *Listen to Your Child* (Penguin 1986), *Rediscover Grammar*, *The English Language* (Penguin 1988), *The Cambridge Encyclopedia of Language*, *Pilgrimage*, *The Cambridge Encyclopedia of the English Language*, *English as a Global Language*, *Language Play* (Penguin 1998) and *The Penguin Dictionary of Language* (Penguin 1999). He is also the editor of the Cambridge family of general encyclopedias.

David Crystal has returned to Holyhead, where he works as a writer, lecturer and consultant on language and linguistics, and a reference books editor. He is also a frequent radio broadcaster. In June 1995 he was awarded the OBE.

Contents

1 | Beginning at the Beginning

Consider Susie.

Susie is 0 years, 0 months, 0 days, and 1 minute old. Life has been quite fraught recently, and there's been a lot of noise about – mainly hers. But now it's time to settle down and take in something of the world around. There is a lot to feel, to smell, to taste, to see and, above all, to hear.

Susie saw nothing of what was going on, in fact, for her eyes were tightly shut for the first few minutes of her birth day. But during that time, she had the chance of hearing around her:
– over a hundred utterances, containing in total
– over 500 words, containing in total
– over 2,000 vowels and consonants.

They were utterances such as these:

It's a girl, Mrs Smith!	Put that on there, will you?
Oh, isn't she gorgeous!	You're lovely, you know that?
O K, I've got her.	Another one, please, nurse.

Once she had stopped crying, there was no way she could shut these sounds out – apart from falling asleep (which came half an hour later) or putting her fingers in her ears (which came two years later). That is the peculiar power of sound, compared with vision. You cannot 'shut your ears', as you can 'shut your eyes'.

Susie has evidently been born into an English-speaking community, so, if she stays within it, she will have to learn the grammar, vocabulary, and pronunciation of many utterances of this kind. To be precise, if she is going to end up speaking the same language as her parents, she needs to learn the following:
– the 20 vowels and 24 consonants of the spoken language, and over 300 ways of combining these sounds into sequences (e.g. $s + p + r$ can be combined in such words as *spring*);
– an adult-speaking vocabulary of around 50,000 words, and an

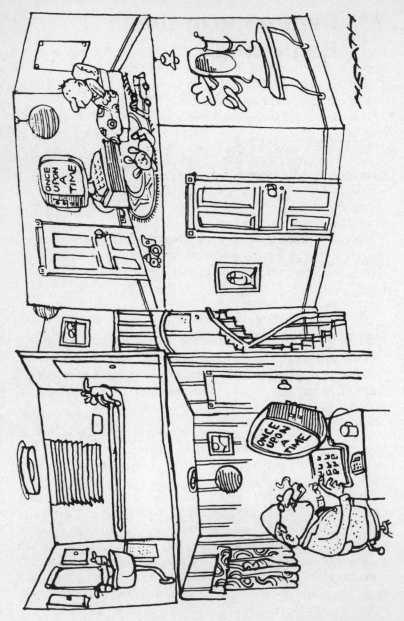

ability to understand the vocabulary of others that may be twice as great;

– around 1,000 rules of grammar, which will tell her how to string words together to make acceptable sentences.

If she had been born into any other language community, things would not have been very different.

Susie has quite a language-learning task in front of her. How will she get on?

Let us jump ahead in time, in the way that only authors can. Susie was tape-recorded talking to her baby-sitter one afternoon in December, when she was four years seven months old. 1,671 days old, to be precise. She's been awake for about 20,000 hours during that time, but only a fraction of this time has been devoted to talking – probably less than a tenth in all. Nonetheless, from one part of the recording came the following remarkable narrative. (Pauses are marked by – .)

Susie: Oh, look, a crab. We seen – we were been to the seaside.

Baby-sitter: Have you?

Susie: We saw cr – fishes and crabs. And we saw a jellyfish, and we had to bury it. And we – we did holding crabs, and we – we holded him in by the spade.

Baby-sitter: Did you?

Susie: Yes, to kill them, so they won't bite our feet.

Baby-sitter: Oh.

Susie: If you stand on them, they hurt you, won't they.

Baby-sitter: They would do. They'd pinch you.

Susie: You'd have to – and we put them under the sand, where the sea was. And they were going to the sea.

Baby-sitter: Mhm.

Susie: And we saw some shells. And we picked them up, and we heard the sea in them. And we saw a crab on a lid. And we saw lots of crabs on the sea side. And I picked the – fishes up – no, the shells, and the feathers from the birds. – And I saw a pig.

Baby-sitter: Gosh, that was fun.

Susie: Yes, and I know a story about pigs.

Baby-sitter: Are you going to tell it to me?

Susie: One – one day they went out to build their houses. One
 built it of straw, one built it of sticks, and one built it of
 bricks. And he – the little busy brother knowed that in the
 woods there lived a big bad wolf, he need nothing else but
 to catch little pigs. So, you know what, one day they went
 out – and – the wolf went slip slosh slip slosh went his feet
 on the ground. Then – let me see, er – now I think – he said
 let me come in, you house of straw. And he said, no no by
 my hair of my chinny-chin-chin, I will not let you come in.
 Then I'll huff, and I'll puff, and I'll puff, and I'll blow your
 house down. So he huffed, and he puffed, and he puffed,
 and he puffed, and he blew the little straw house all to
 pieces. Then away went the little brother to his brother's
 house of sticks . . .

And so the monologue continues, for nearly two minutes. The
story-line of course comes from one of her favourite bed-time
sagas, and she has evidently been a keen listener. She reproduces
several of its phrases very accurately – not only the wolf's words,
but some of the story-teller's style, such as 'Away went . . .' She
also dramatizes the narrative – though you can't tell from the
above transcription: 'big bad wolf' is said with long, drawn-out
vowels; and the huffing and puffing is accompanied by a great
puffing out of the cheeks, and an increased presence, as Susie draws
herself up to her full height – all 42" of it. You can easily tell, from
her version, how her parents must have acted out the story.

On the other hand, this is definitely Susie's story, not the book's.
If you compare her words with those of the original, there are all
kinds of partial correspondences, but hardly anything is repeated
exactly as it was. For instance, the book does not begin with that
opening line; the phrase *the little busy brother* isn't used there; and
she puffs far more than the wolf does. Susie may have learned the
events of the story off by heart, and several of its words and
phrases, but it is largely her own grammar which is stringing
them together. It is also very much her style: at the time, the use
of the *you know what* and *let me see* were definite 'Susie-isms'.

As you can tell from the pauses and the rephrasings, Susie's
speech isn't perfectly fluent. It's rather jerky at times, and sometimes it comes out in such a rush that it's difficult to follow. Her

pronunciation, too, is somewhat immature – she says [kwab] for *crab*, for instance, and [bwuvə] for *brother*.* And she has the child-like preference for joining sentences using *and* – the commonest linking word among children, from around age 3 onwards. She is also still sorting out some points of grammar, especially in relation to the way verbs are used: she says *knowed* instead of *knew*, *we seen* alongside *we saw*, *we did hold* instead of *we held*, and there is the interesting *we were been*, with its confusion of tenses.

But the overwhelming impression we receive from the story, as from the whole dialogue, is one of great competence and confidence. Susie is having no difficulty keeping her end up in this conversation; indeed, if anyone is having trouble keeping up, it is the baby-sitter! Look at the strength of her sea-shore vocabulary, for instance. Or the complex grammatical constructions which are so casually introduced in passing. A sentence such as *If you stand on them, they hurt you* displays a considerable amount of grammatical skill: the sentence has a 'main clause' (*they hurt you*) and a 'subordinate clause' (*if . . .*); the word order is correct; the verbs (*stand, hurt*) are being used to express the subtle meaning of a 'habitual' or 'timeless' action; and the pronouns (*you, they*) are being used accurately (a few months before, she would probably have said *them hurt you*). She has also mastered the difficult 'logic' of sentences beginning with *if*, which expresses the relationship of cause and effect.

This isn't the only example. Several other sentences show a similar level of complexity. Try disentangling the grammatical elements of *to kill them, so they won't bite our feet* and *we put them under the sand, where the sea was*. Or, if you know, or happen to be learning, a foreign language, translate these sentences into the grammar of that language, and you'll quickly develop a sense of the complex construction involved.

Susie was in no way an exceptional child. She was bright, certainly, but not precocious. There had been no surprises in her milestones of development – crawling, walking, and so on. She

---

* Throughout this book, the sounds of speech will be transcribed using the normal letters of the alphabet, along with a few special symbols, which will be explained as they appear. Wherever I quote an actual pronunciation, the fact will be signalled through the use of square brackets, as above.

lived in a middle-class, middle-income family, along with her father (a teacher), mother (an ex-nurse), big brother (2 years older), a hamster, a cat, a TV and a radio. Someone, or something, was always switched on, so she heard a lot of language, but no more than you might expect from many a family home. She also had a very friendly, outgoing personality – a great asset, when it comes to language learning – but there again, any pre-school playgroup will immediately display a dozen extrovert charmers of this kind. Her conversational skills are impressive, after only 20,000 hours of life, but they are by no means unique. Talking to her friend, Joanne, you would hardly be able to tell them apart.

'They grow up so quickly' is a remark all parents make about their children, sooner or later, and it applies as much to the rate at which they acquire language as to any other aspect of development. It is the enormous speed at which children move, as they travel along the language acquisition road, which has impressed everyone – not only their parents and relatives, but even the hard-nosed group of psychologists and linguists who have specialized in the field of child language acquisition, a field which is often called 'developmental psycholinguistics'. It is easy to think of the children as linguistic racing cars, roaring away on the grid at the start, then zooming ahead, each lap adding to their abilities in the use of sounds, grammar, and vocabulary. Analogies can damage your health, but this is not a bad one really. For, as we shall see, the children, like the cars, move at different speeds, but always in the same general direction. Their progress fluctuates greatly as they encounter the many obstacles in their way. Certain parts of the circuit are straightforward, and taken at speed; other parts are tortuous, and require careful negotiation. Some take longer to leave the starting grid than they should, but once they are away they catch up well before the race is over. By contrast, there are a few – a sadly neglected few – who never leave the grid at all; and a further group who begin the race but never finish it, because an accident intervenes. We shall discuss these, the language-impaired children, in Chapter 7.

The acquisition of our mother-tongue is the most significant act of learning of our early life, perhaps of our whole life. Once we have language at our disposal, we have a key which will unlock many doors. We have permanent access to the records of our past. We can contribute in full measure to the developments of the present. We can plan our future. Language acquisition is thus a subject which pre-eminently deserves our understanding, and it is not surprising that it has these days become a major field of academic research. Yet, people do sometimes ask, 'What is there to research into?' When the *Journal of Child Language* was first published, in the 1970s, a correspondent wrote to me, as the editor, and asked why it was needed. 'Children's language is hardly a complicated matter,' he wrote. 'Surely all that children do is imitate their parents. Why is that so surprising?'

Of course, if that was all there was to it, there would indeed be little need for a research journal, and this book would stop here. But one of the first findings of child language researchers in fact demonstrated that simple explanations of this kind do not work. Children do sometimes imitate their parents and others around them, as we shall see, but a great deal of what they say could not possibly have come from the language of adults. Look again at the Susie dialogue. Which adults did Susie copy in order to say *knowed*, *holded*, and the other immature forms scattered throughout her speech? None, of course. Susie has thought these up for herself. Some time previously, she must have worked it out that there is a difference between such pairs of words as *walk/walked* and *jump/jumped*, and assumed that the same thing should happen for *know* and *hold*. And not just these: at other points in the recording she also said *taked* and *bringed*; and a few months before, she said *goned*, *seed*, *putted*, and many more. She seems to have learned a 'rule' which says: if you want to form a past tense, add *ed* to the present tense. It's a rule which works well for the majority of English verbs, but there are a few hundred (the 'irregular' verbs) to which it doesn't apply. Now that she's $4\frac{1}{2}$, she's evidently managed to sort out some of these exceptions: *saw*, *put*, and *heard*. But there is still clear evidence of the rule which, a few months before, she invented for herself.

She is not alone. All children, in all languages, do similar things. If you know a child between 3 and $4\frac{1}{2}$ years of age, you will hear many such rules in action. Not just verbs, but nouns, adjectives, and other aspects of language are manipulated in the same way. Nouns form their plurals by 'adding an *s*', it seems: thus, *cat/cats*, *dog/dogs*, *horse/horses*. Children find this to be another excellent rule, and they then use it for all nouns: thus we encounter *mouse/mouses*, *sheep/sheeps*, and *foot/foots*. Once again, we see the child's own reasoning in action. These forms aren't used by adults, so the possibility of imitation does not arise.

My correspondent's simple explanation of the way children learn language won't, then, stand up. Children are not parrots: they take an active role in their own linguistic future. The situation is plainly far more complicated than might appear at first sight, and it is this complexity which has motivated all the research by developmental psycholinguists. What, then, have these scholars discovered? What can be said about the way language acquisition takes place? When does the process start? When does it end? Are there such things as 'linguistic milestones'? What parts of the task pose particular problems? Can we, as parents and relatives, help our children in any way, or should we leave well alone? These are intricate and fascinating questions, and after some twenty years of modern scientific research, answers to all of them are beginning to emerge. It is research to which everyone can contribute, incidentally, once they train themselves to listen to the linguistic behaviour of children in a cool, systematic manner.

But this book does not aim to turn parents into researchers. Its intention is simply to provide some insight into the course of language acquisition, and thus to contribute to the sense of satisfaction which comes from knowing as much as possible about how our children 'work', and the pride we feel when we recognize their achievements. We take great pleasure from observing how they take one step, then two, then three . . . or place one brick on top of another, then a second, then a third . . . In the world of language, many more such prospects appear, as new vocabulary emerges, pronunciation matures, and sentences get longer and more complex. We thrill at the sound of a child's first word; but no less fascinating, as we shall see, is the emergence of the first intonation pattern, the first two-word sentence, the first use of pronouns, or the first use of *and*. The more we know about the details of language development, the more there is to delight in. I recall one linguist arriving at the office in paroxysms of delight, because his child, as he put it, had that morning 'correctly used a relative clause in subject position'! Such sophisticated terminology comes only from those who read grammar books in bed. But we can all share in the insights these statements reflect, once we start listening carefully not just to *what* children say, but to *how* they say it.

Feature 1 | How much do children say in a day?

On Monday 19 June 1972, Klaus Wagner, a child language researcher from the University of Dortmund, West Germany, got up very early, in order to get to 9½-year-old Theresa's house, before she awoke. That day, she woke up just after 7. At 7.06, a mini-microphone transmitter was sewn on to her clothes. There were no wires linking this with the tape recorder, so she was free to move around wherever she wanted. From that moment on, everything she said was recorded, as she progressed through her day.

She had breakfast, packed her bag and was driven to school. Some time was spent chatting before school began, and then she was into her lessons (arithmetic and language), with the usual morning break. There was a prize-giving that day, and this was followed by the drive home. At the house, she helped clear things away, read some letters, and talked about her work. Then she picked some gooseberries, and played with some friends – catching the cat, dressing up, clowns, ballet and kidnappers. Next came a late lunch, and more gooseberry picking; then homework, coffee, and putting toys away. More play followed – this time it included tree-climbing, playing on the grass, hopping on the patio, skipping, and being gold thieves and investigators. She watched some television, had dinner, watched some more television, and finally went to bed just after 8.30. The recording session was ended at 8.30.

Altogether, 804 minutes of Theresa's life were recorded on tape that day. Later, Wagner meticulously went through the tape, and transcribed everything that Theresa had said. He then counted the number of words she used. How much did she say in that day? Before giving you the total number of words, you might like to pause and reflect on the situation, and arrive at your own estimate. If you have a pen handy, jot your total down in this box, before looking at the next page.

```
┌──────────────┐
│              │
└──────────────┘
```

What do you think? 3,000? 5,000? 10,000? A lively 9½-year-old, remember, and a very full day. 15,000 perhaps? On the other hand, she did spend a fair amount of time listening in class, and presumably doing many things not necessarily requiring any speech. Perhaps only 10,000 then? Or are you thinking about a much lower – or higher – total?

If higher, you were right. Theresa's total was an amazing 28,142!

You don't *have* to be an expert to get this wrong. But when I was first asked this question, I put down a confident estimate of 15,000. How wrong can you be!

The figure of 28,142 refers to word *tokens* – that is, the number of actual words used, regardless of how much repetition there was. For instance, Theresa must have used the German word for *the* hundreds of times that day, and each instance was counted once. What would have been the total if all of these repetitions had not been separately counted, if only the number of *different* words were tallied? The total is much less, of course, but it is still unexpectedly high: Theresa used 3,825 word *types* – that is, number of different words.

Here's another remarkable fact about Theresa. From the 804 minutes of recording, Wagner subtracted the amount of time when others were talking, and the amount of time when no one was talking. That left a total of 191 minutes. The time it took Theresa to say everything she had to say was a little over 3 hours! With a little help from a calculator, you can work out that she must have been speaking, on average, at a rate of over 9,000 words per hour – 155·5 words per minute, 2½ per second!

You're perhaps thinking, at this point, that Theresa isn't a typical 9½-year-old. Maybe the researchers had stumbled upon a particularly bright or verbal child. The mother was an ex-teacher, and the father a university lecturer, so perhaps they were fostering a highly 'verbal' environment which would make this an exceptional total? And how far is the high figure of this age typical of other ages?

These were Wagner's first thoughts also. He therefore arranged for similar recordings to be made of children from different backgrounds, and of different ages, and over a dozen studies were

carried out between 1974 and 1979. Another full day's recording
was carried out on Friday 20 January 1978, from 7.24 a.m. to
10 p.m. – a total of 876 minutes. Kai was also 9½, the child of
upper working class parents: his mother was a landlady, and his
father was a draughtsman who had died when Kai was 3. Kai's
school day was similar to Theresa's, but his playtime was rather
different – playing Monopoly, driving a go-cart, playing in a
Citroën 2 CV, soldering, drawing, making a tassel, a memory
game, and watching television. His total was 25,401 word
tokens – less than Theresa's, but still extremely high. He also
spoke much more slowly than Theresa: it took him nearly 4½
hours to say all this, at a much lower rate of 97 words per
minute.

The other studies took various amounts of time, so to aid
comparison Wagner calculated the totals in terms of a standard
unit of 12 hours. The youngest child in the sample was aged 1½;
the oldest was nearly 15. You can, if you like, try to guess the
totals for these ages, or for the years in between, but I would
not advise it! Here is what the research team found.

	Total number of words (i.e. tokens)	Number of different words (i.e. types)
Katrin, 1 year 5 months	13,800	1,860
Nicole, 1 year 8 months	11,700	not available
Andreas, 2 years 1 month	20,200	2,210
Carsten, 3 years 6 months	37,700	4,790
Gabi, 5 years 4 months	30,600	2,490
Frederik, 8 years 7 months	24,700	3,960
Roman, 9 years 2 months	24,400	3,630
Markus, 11 years 4 months	37,200	5,020
Christiane, 12 years 2 months	22,600	3,580
Axel, 14 years 10 months	22,900	3,040

There is a noticeable jump between the two youngest children
and the rest – but who would have guessed that a 1½-year-old
would produce 10,000 words in a day and know nearly 2,000
different words? After age 2, the figure fluctuates a great deal,
and at least two of the children seem genuinely exceptional.
Markus found himself involved in two very intensive conversations – making a car and using a microscope. And Carsten – what

a 3½-year-old she must have been! – has a grandmother always available to talk to.

Of course, it is possible to tinker with these figures, to obtain slightly different results. A lot depends on how you define the word 'word' in the first place. In English, for example, would you count *it's* as one word or two? And would you call *walk*, *walks*, *walked* and *walking* 'different' words (as did the German researchers) or different forms of the 'same' word?

The results of this project were published in 1985. The overall conclusion is unavoidable: these German children speak an average of between 20,000 and 30,000 words a day, from as early as their third year of life. They also have a daily active vocabulary of around 3,000 different words. The speed at which they speak ranges from a leisurely 46·2 words per minute, for the youngest child, to 187·5 wpm for the oldest. A rate of 100 wpm is achieved as early as 3½, and this increases to around 150 wpm once they go to school.

What would the corresponding figures be for English, I wonder? I know of no such count, but I would expect the figures to be even higher, mainly because many of the compound words of German would be replaced by word sequences in English – *Einbahnstraße*, for instance, is translated by *one-way street*.

Word counts of this kind are not difficult to do if you have the recording equipment, the motivation and, above all, the time. But how many of us have all of that? The time factor is especially important. You won't get reliable results if you record only a short period of speech. The children may be shy, so that the figures will come out too low; or they may be stimulated too much by the microphone, so that the figures will be too high. The adults around will almost certainly try to make the children talk a lot, if they know the recorder is on for only a short period, and that will mess up the results too. The only way of getting these influences to cancel out is to use a long period of recording time – preferably, most of a day. And that's only the beginning of the exercise. You then have to allow several days simply to listen to the tapes and get the words down accurately. And that means listening repeatedly to parts of the tape where the child's voice is competing with motor cars, Lego and maybe even Concorde. Equipment, motivation, time . . . oh yes, and a placid temperament, too.

All parents like to keep a photograph album of their child's development. The linguistic equivalent is an archive of tape recordings of the child's speech. It's easy to do, as long as you are organized, and remember to take a few basic precautions.

1. *Tape recorders* The cost and size of the tape recorder is not a crucial factor. Nor is the distinction between cassette and reel-to-reel machines (unless you intend to do some editing – see Point 10). Of course, as with cameras, the better the machine the better the recording quality. But these days most portable machines are perfectly adequate for voice recordings.

Bear in mind that you need an electricity supply! If a mains supply is always available, no problem. But if you intend to record in places where access to the mains is difficult (e.g. out in the country, in a bathroom, or if you're having to follow the child around a lot), then a machine powered by batteries may be easier. However, batteries run out. So, before a recording, make sure that you've checked them – recharged them, if that's possible, or replaced them. (It's worth investing in one of those devices which tell you how much power is left in a battery.)

Anticipate the problem of locating the material once you've recorded it. If possible, use a machine with a number counter, otherwise you'll have great difficulty finding your place on the tape from one recording to the next. It isn't as easy as turning the pages in a photo album. Use tapes which are as short as possible – 15 or 20 minute cassettes, or a 5" reel. The longer the tape, the longer you'll take to find your way to a place upon it, when you want to listen again to a recording.

If your machine has a choice of tape speeds, choose one speed and remember to use it for all recordings – otherwise as you listen from one session to the next, the child will sound normal one minute and like Donald Duck the next! If you intend to do some editing (see Point 10), use the highest possible speed; otherwise, a middle speed (such as $3\frac{3}{4}$) will do. A very low speed on a cheap machine should be avoided, as it often doesn't control the movement of the tape smoothly and the voices come to sound as if the owners were seasick.

2. *Microphones* This piece of equipment needs careful thought. Some microphones pick up sound equally from all round them (they are 'omnidirectional'). Some pick up sound from front and back, but not from the sides ('bidirectional'). Others pick up sound only from the direction in which the microphone is pointing (they are 'unidirectional'). All have their value.

Omnidirectional mikes are useful if a child is moving around a lot while the recording is being made. They're also very handy if several people are being recorded, such as a group of children, or a parent and child who are at different places in the room. The main problem with them is that all sound in the vicinity is recorded equally: if there are other voices you would rather exclude (as in a classroom), or background noise which would interfere (such as traffic noise outside), this microphone could cause difficulties.

Unidirectional mikes help to eliminate these problems, but of course they work well only if the child is in one place, such as in a cot, in front of a book, or playing at a table. If more than one person is involved in the recording, also, care must be taken to ensure that both voices get their fair share of the microphone. Bidirectional mikes give somewhat greater flexibility, but there are still several restrictions on movement.

Often, you have no choice about which microphone to use, because it is already *inside* the tape recorder. This is increasingly the case these days, now that radio-cassette recorders have become so popular.

All these problems are avoided if you use a radio microphone, but these are quite expensive, and you usually see them only in research projects. This is a device which can be clipped on to the child's clothing, or hung round the neck. It has a small aerial, but no wire connects it to the tape recorder, which may be some distance away. The child can move freely, therefore, but the microphone stays at the same distance from the voice, so that you get an even recording quality.

3. *Where to put the equipment* The microphone should be placed as near as possible to the child's mouth without it becoming obtrusive. There is a real problem here for machines which have an internal microphone. It can be very awkward putting the whole works inside a cot, for instance, whereas a free microphone linked by a wire to the recorder can be tied to the bars of the cot quite easily. At older ages, children can easily be distracted by a large machine whirring away in front of them, whereas a small microphone can be partly hidden, and is usually quickly forgotten about.

People sometimes think that if the child can see the tape recorder, the whole purpose of the recording is destroyed. There is certainly a problem here for researchers, who have to ensure that their recordings are natural and spontaneous, if they are to reach the right conclusions about the normal development of speech. But for everyday domestic recording, this isn't an issue, any more than is the fact that the child can see the camera while you take a photograph. We all know that surreptitiously taken snapshots can be delightful, and the same applies to tape recordings. But no one considers a photograph to be valueless just because the child knew it was being taken.

4. *When to make the recording* In theory, it can be any time. In practice, it's wise to get into a routine, for your own sake, as much as the child's. If there's no routine, you'll forget to do it, or put it off until tomorrow . . . and tomorrow . . . and tomorrow . . . The recordings should be at regular intervals, to ensure that you capture most of the changes as they occur. This is where the parallel with photography breaks down, of course. You can plan your visual record of the child to a considerable extent: if you go out for the day, you take your camera, knowing that new and photographable things are likely to happen. But you cannot plan your auditory record in this way: who knows whether, today, the child is going to say something new or interesting?

It isn't practicable to record everything. Even the largest research projects have to rely on samples. Life isn't long enough to listen a second time to all that a child says, and as most of the utterances involve a great deal of repetition, there would hardly be a point. So, the first and most important thing to decide is *how often* to record. Daily, weekly, fortnightly, monthly . . . ?

There isn't really a simple answer. Language acquisition doesn't proceed evenly, at so many sounds, words and constructions per day. It moves in fits and starts. One week, very little might happen; the next, several developments occur. To catch these unexpected spurts, some research surveys sample every few days. But for most domestic purposes, once a month is usually enough to capture the main trends in development. Choose a date or a day (e.g. the 1st, or the first Sunday) and stick to it as your recording day. Alter it only if there are problems (e.g. illness, unexpected visitors). Remember that if there's extra excitement about (such as a birthday party), you may be faced with recording difficulties.

What time during the day? Avoid the late afternoon and evening, when the child gets tired (though young children's 'bedroom monologues', before they go to sleep, are often quite fascinating). Avoid mealtimes, because of the noise. Avoid times when the child would rather be doing something else (such as watching a favourite TV programme). Otherwise, any time.

5. *Where to record* Anywhere that the child has settled down to play happily. The setting should be familiar. Young children tend to become deafeningly silent in new surroundings. Bring the tape recorder to the child, not the other way round. Check for background noise before you begin – not just by listening, but by recording the sound of the silence. It is remarkable how often you hear things on the tape that you hadn't noticed through the air (e.g. a washing machine throbbing away in another room). If at all possible, turn the unwanted noise off.

6. *How much to record* The main limiting factor here is a purely practical one. For every minute you record, you must find a minute to play it back. An audio tape recording isn't like a photo album, which can be quickly flipped through, or a video recording which can be speeded up. The saddest sight in language acquisition is a shelf full of dusty tapes that no one has the time to listen to. You mustn't let yourself get into that position. If the child is talking fairly constantly during the recording, a *minute* is usually plenty. If the talk is more sporadic, then perhaps five minutes. But

longer recordings should be avoided, unless it's an exceptional occasion, such as a birthday.

7. *What to record* With babies, more or less any typical vocal output will do – but it is as well to avoid those vocalizations which might be described, technically, as 'screaming the house down'. With older children, the ideal is to obtain samples of 'free conversation' – something which proves increasingly easy to obtain as the child grows older. Anything which prompts such a conversation is of value, such as a set of toys, or pictures in a book. But there are a few difficulties to look out for.

If you are using toys as a stimulus, make sure they are quiet, otherwise the noise will obscure the language on the tape. Everyday toys which cause a problem are boxes of bricks, or sets of cars. Bricks *will* keep falling over, and cars keep crashing. The simple expedient of a thick cloth (if playing on the table) or rug (if on the floor) can help, but they often don't pass the child's censorship. Cars run rottenly on rugs.

The main problem with pictures is that they greatly restrict the range of the young child's responses. There's a marked tendency for the utterances to be simple names or descriptions (*There's a car*, *It's a circus*), and some areas of language will be used to the exclusion of others. The present tense, for instance (e.g. *is*, *are*, *is jumping*, *jumps*), will be everywhere, with other tense forms missing. You can get round this problem to some extent, by prodding the child with questions and comments which take attention away from the pictures (e.g. *Do you remember we saw a lion once?*), but this is quite tricky to do naturally, when you (the adult) know you're being recorded, and it may not always work. If you do use pictures, try to find ones where several things are happening (such as a busy seaside scene, or a shopping centre), so that there's more chance of catching the child's interest.

Free conversation is best, on a topic which you know interests the child. Topics which usually work include something that happened on a recent TV programme, the imaginary adventures of a favourite cuddly toy, or talk about household routines, such as getting tea ready, or gardening (but not, say, getting ready for bed, which the child may not want to talk about because of its bad vibes!).

When you've made the recording, try to find a moment to listen to it later in the day – not for fun, but to see if it's come out all right. You may have forgotten to press the 'record' button at the same time as 'play', or the cassette may have jammed, or you may have had a power cut, and never noticed. Also, this gives you the chance to see whether the content of the recording is intelligible. You'll often find that a dialogue which you understood perfectly well when you were with the child becomes incomprehensible when you hear it on tape. It's because you can't see what was being talked about. You may therefore need to jot a few notes down about what the child was saying, or referring to, while it's reasonably fresh in your mind. If you do, sellotape the notes to the tape box, otherwise they'll fall out one day and get lost.

8. *Keep your records straight* 'How old was Jimmy when we took that photo?' 'I've no idea – two? three?' This conversation happens often enough with photographs, when we forget to keep a note of when we took them. The same problem arises with tape recordings, only in more severe form, because there are very few clues about age in a child's voice quality. To avoid it, you must resolve to keep your records straight, from the outset.

There's not much to do. Choose tapes or cassettes which give you space to write the contents on the outside. If necessary, stick a piece of blank paper to the outside of the box, and use that. Write the child's name, the date of the recording, and the length of the recording, and (if there's a number counter) where on the tape it is located. Use abbreviations to save space. Use ' for minutes, and if necessary " for seconds (e.g. 2'30" = 'two minutes and thirty seconds').

It's worth adding a note of how old the child was too (to avoid awkward subtraction sums later, e.g. the recording was made on 11.3.85; she was born on 8.6.79; how old was she?). A common way of abbreviating ages is to write the year and month in numbers, separated by a semi-colon (e.g. 2;6 = two years and six months, 3;11 = three years and eleven months). I shall be using this abbreviation myself throughout this book. If you want to be more precise, the number of days can be added following a full stop (e.g. 2;6.21 = two years, six months, twenty-one days).

Try to make sure there's space to add a note about the context of the recording, e.g. 'talking to mum about the circus'. This is the equivalent of labelling your photographs. It'll help you remember what your favourite extracts are, one day.

Here are some entries from one box, where this procedure was followed:

```
000–093 Mary and dad, doll's house play.   13.12.84  2;6  2'.
095–190 Mary and mum, doll's house play. 13.1.85   2;7  2'.
195–290 Mary and mum, making cakes.      12.2.85   2;8  2'.
```

9. *Keep an eye on the tape* When you're approaching the end of one side of tape, estimate if there's enough space left to complete your next recording.

When you reach the end, it's much more convenient to start a second tape, from the viewpoint of later play-back. Don't record on the second side (unless you're having to economize). If you record on both sides, and the extract you want to play is on the second side, you'll have the chore of winding through the first side of the tape before you can get anywhere – and the subsequent chore of rewinding, so that the tape is 'right way round' inside its box. It's a chore all right, as evidenced by the many tapes which are left un-rewound in their boxes. But it needs to be done, for technical as well as social reasons. If cassettes are not properly rewound, the tape can lose its tension, with a risk of loss of quality, or even damage (if it gets all chewed up inside the recorder). And marriages can be at risk if such things are not done. To be mated with someone who leaves a reel back-to-front in a box, or a cassette half wound back, is only slightly less dangerous than finding that their habit of squeezing toothpaste tubes is different from yours!

So, single-sided recordings are simpler than double-sided ones, though more expensive in terms of money and space. Either way, remember to number each box in sequence, and store them safely – away from dust, heat, damp, and sources of magnetic interference (such as a hi-fi loudspeaker).

GOVERNMENT HEALTH WARNING:
TAPE RECORDING YOUR CHILD CAN BE DANGEROUS

As every psycholinguist knows, life is full of wonderful auditory moments, most of which take place when the tape recorder is switched off. It is therefore very important, if you intend to record your child, to spend several days in retreat first, developing an appropriately calm frame of mind. Only in this way will you control the desire to scream which wells up within all of us when, after several minutes of fruitless recording, you glumly turn off the machine, to be immediately rewarded with the desired utterance. This is known as Murphy's Law No. 861.

10. *Editing* Tape editing is a fairly specialized activity, which most people haven't the time to do; but if you become an enthusiast, you may want to try it. You can then record longer stretches of speech, extract the best bits, and string them together to make a more organized and interesting tape. There are often long periods of silence in a spontaneous conversation, or places where all you can hear is the sound of bricks and the child's heavy breathing. With some editing equipment, you can cut these out.

It isn't possible to edit material from cassettes without a second tape recorder and special linking equipment. With reels of tape, it's not difficult, as long as you use a small editing kit. Typically, this consists of a box in which there is a safety razor blade, some sticky tape, and a device for holding your tape in place. In the diagrams below, a length of tape is shown, with a piece marked which you want to cut out (A–B).

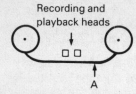

Recording and playback heads

1. Cut tape at A

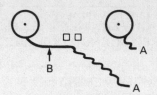

2. Pull tape through
   until you reach B.
   Cut tape at B

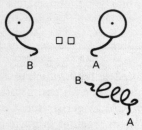

3. Bring ends A and
   B together, using your
   editing kit. Throw
   away the unwanted
   tape, before the child
   tries to eat it

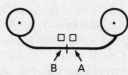

4. Once A and B are
   stuck together, you shouldn't
   be able to 'hear the join'

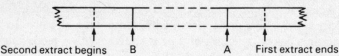

Second extract begins   B   A   First extract ends

5. Make your cuts (A and B) a little *after*
   the first extract ends, and a little *before*
   the second extract begins, to avoid
   mistakes

1. Let the tape play through the machine until you reach point A.
2. Mark the place on the outside of the tape using a felt-tip pen (the outside is usually the side nearest to you as you face the front of the machine). It is important to put this mark in the right place, otherwise you may cut through a part of the tape you want to keep! If you are going to do some editing, record your tape at a fast speed, to allow room for error. If the tape is travelling at $7\frac{1}{2}$ (or 15) inches per second, you are much more likely to place your cut correctly than if the speed is $3\frac{3}{4}$. With tape travelling at only $1\frac{7}{8}$, it would be impossible to make a correct cut.
3. Insert this section of tape into the tape-holder, and make a clean cut at point A.
4. Leave the right-hand section of tape fastened in the holder, but release the left-hand piece.
5. Let the tape run on, spilling out on to the floor, until you reach point B.
6. Repeat steps 2 and 3 for point B.
7. The piece of tape to be discarded will fall on the floor. Leave the left-hand section of tape fastened in the holder.
8. The two pieces of tape are now opposite each other in the holder, and ready to be joined. If your cutting has been neat, the two sides should match. Place a piece of sticky tape over the join, and press it firmly against the two sides of tape. Use the razor blade to trim the edges, so that they do not overlap the width of the tape.
9. Release the tape from the holder, and wind it back on to the spool. Then play the edited section of tape through, to see what kind of job you have done. You'll see the edited section pass through from one spool to the other, but you shouldn't be able to hear the join.

For your first efforts, leave a little space on the tape between the end of the first extract and point A, and between point B and the beginning of the second extract. This will give you some leeway, in case you put the cutting mark in the wrong place. With practice, you'll find you can do without these spaces.

Lucy, aged 5½, decided to play at being a waitress. She spent a busy twenty minutes arranging a table and chair, toy plates and cups, and a miscellaneous supply of cutlery. It took so long, because she insisted on using all the available pieces, even though there were only four places at the table. One customer that day would have had the choice of four knives, three forks, and six assorted spoons!

Once she was satisfied with her arrangement, she looked around for customers. A teddy, a panda, and two dolls were tried out in turn at the table, then rejected as being unworthy to dine at her establishment – doubtless because they were improperly dressed. She looked around for a better class of customer, and found one reluctant diner behind a newspaper in the next room. The diner explained that he was very busy, but he would play just for a minute. The conversation then proceeded along the following lines.

Dad: What do you want to play, then?
Lucy: I'll be the waitress, and you have to eat in my shop. You come in, and sit down, and I can come and see you.
(*Dad acts his part obediently. Over walks Lucy, clutching an imaginary notebook and pencil.*)
Lucy: Good afternoon.
Dad: Good afternoon.
Lucy: What do you want to eat?
Dad: Ooh, I'd like some cornflakes, and some sausages, please.
Lucy: We haven't got any sausages.
Dad: Oh dear. Well, let me see . . . Have you got any steak?
(*There is a silence, while Lucy considers this possibility with enormous gravity. Finally, she allows it.*)
Lucy: Yes. We got steak.
Dad: I'll have some steak, then.

Lucy: O.K. 'Bye.
(*She turns to go, but Dad calls her back.*)
Dad: Hey, hold on a minute. You can't rush off like that. If a customer asks for steak, you have to ask him 'How would you like your steak?' That's very important, if you're going to be a waitress.
Lucy: Oh. (*Pauses.*) How would you like your steak?
Dad: I'll have mine well done.
Lucy (*trotting off to the kitchen*): O.K. We'll do the best we can!

Comment

Lucy has learned the basic, literal interpretation of the phrase *well done*: something 'has been performed successfully'. But she doesn't seem to have met the special sense, where *done* means 'cooked', and *well* means 'for a long time'. By itself, this is not very surprising. The phrase is restricted to the world of cooking, or similar situations (such as referring to a sunburnt back on a beach). What makes it a tricky piece of language acquisition is the fact that it is used idiomatically. You have to learn it 'as a whole', along with the other technical terms for cooking steak. The opposites of *well done* are not *badly done* or *briefly done*, but *rare*, *medium*, and suchlike.

What makes the story linguistically interesting is that it is so typical of the kind of 'decoding' problem which children have to cope with increasingly at around age 6. This is an age when social and linguistic horizons are rapidly broadening (as we shall be discussing in Chapter 6). They are encountering a wider range of styles and dialects, both colloquial and specialized, especially as a result of their new patterns of work and play in school. The idioms of speech flood in around them. One child returned home from school very worried about his teacher being hungry: it transpired that the teacher had been heard to say she *hadn't got a sausage*!

The problem period lasts only for about a year. Soon after 7, most children have worked it out that, in language, 'things are not always as they seem'. *To kick the bucket* does not always mean 'to kick the bucket'. To refer to *sausages* doesn't always mean you're talking about sausages. 'Hmm', one can imagine a child thinking, 'this language learning business is trickier than I thought'. But it's not long before they become wise in the ways of language, and learn to be suspicious of sentences. They soon begin their own kind of linguistic tampering, as they start making puns, riddles, and jokes out of the raw material of sentences. And the most dreaded period of language acquisition dawns before the parents: the age of 'knock, knock' and other jokes (illustrated, if you can bear it, on p. 185).

Ages and stages: a word of warning

Often, throughout this book, I shall talk about stages of language development, and tie these in with particular ages. A certain type of sound is said to emerge between 6 and 9 months. A certain number of words are thought to be acquired by 18 months. Between 2 and 2½, speech is said to display certain kinds of sentence pattern.

None of these time periods should be taken too literally. They don't take account of whether your child is a 'fast developer' or a 'slow developer', for instance. All such dates are averages, based on what has been discovered from the study of several children. To say that something happens between 6 and 9 months doesn't mean that all children start promptly on the first day of the first month and finish promptly on the last day of the second. Always mentally add such phrases as 'more or less' and 'in most children' before any language acquisition date.

Above all, you mustn't think that because *your* child isn't producing sounds, words, or sentences by an expected time, you must drop everything and send out an emergency call for speech therapy. There is an enormous amount of individual variation in language development, and a delay of a few weeks can be perfectly normal. Of course, if a delay becomes a matter of several months, then it would be as well to seek specialized advice (see p. 218); but fortunately that's not very common.

The reason for this note of caution is that the field of language acquisition research is still quite new. The first systematic studies, using modern techniques, were carried out only in the 1960s. The subject is nowadays very popular, but studying children's language is always very intricate and time-consuming, so progress is slow. All generalizations have to be viewed with caution, therefore. In particular, in this book we shall be talking largely about the acquisition of standard English: if your child is learning another mother-tongue, or a regional dialect, you may find that the age ranges given do not exactly apply.

2 | The First Year

When does the process of language acquisition start? It's widely thought that the significant time is around the end of the first year, when children produce their 'first words'. 'He's started to talk today!' is the kind of happy remark parents often make. And in a way, the remark is true. There *is* something special about the first intelligible word a child produces. It's an exciting day when the child officially joins the speech community. There ought to be a badge to commemorate it.

But despite all the excitement, the first word doesn't in fact mark the beginning of a child's language learning. It is the result of a great deal of hard work on the part of both parents and children that has gone on throughout the first year of life. It is the climax of a complex series of linguistic developments which begin at birth – or, as we shall see, even before.

What kinds of development are involved? Let's begin with a general observation. In order to communicate with someone, using spoken language, three abilities need to be present. Obviously, you need to be able to make sounds and string them together into intelligible utterances. Less obviously, you also need to be able to perceive sounds, and understand the meaning of the utterances the other person makes. And, least obviously, you need to know how to interact with that person – how to hold a conversation. By 12 months, children have become quite sophisticated in all three areas.

Making sounds

A baby's ability to make sounds alters enormously between birth and 12 months, so we need to divide the period up into 'stages', to see what is going on. You won't be able to hear a clear division between each stage, of course. Language development is a

"Mum! The baby can talk—he just said 'necrophilia'."

gradual, continuous process. From one day to the next, there seems to be no change at all – and then suddenly you notice that the child is doing something different. How many 'different' kinds of vocal behaviour can we observe in a child during the first year?

Five, I think. I have to say 'I think', because the changes are so subtle that researchers quite often disagree about when they take place, and how many types of change there are. I've heard some splendid rows about these matters at child language research conferences! Still, you shouldn't have too much difficulty distinguishing the following types of infant vocalization.

Stage 1 (0–8 weeks): Basic biological noises

The coughing and spluttering which first issues from the mouth of a new-born child is natural enough: there is a lot of mess about, and a lot of breathing to be done. So too is the raucous, rhythmical crying which quickly follows, which opens the lungs, and arouses the instincts of the mother. Her baby is alive, but in distress. It needs comforting.

Over the first few weeks of life, the vocal sounds made by a baby directly reflect its biological state and activities. States of hunger, pain, or discomfort cause crying and fussing – 'reflexive' noises. Activities include the noises made while the baby breathes, eats, excretes, and performs other bodily movements to do with survival – 'vegetative' noises. Feeding, for example, gives rise to the sounds of sucking, swallowing, coughing, burping, and being sick. Also, while feeding, you can sometimes hear quiet, low-pitched sounds – an early form of cooing. But when not engaged in any of these activities, the baby stays silent.

Infant reflexive cries have been studied in detail. The normal 'basic' cry is a series of pulses, each pulse being about one second long, and separated by a very brief pause while the baby breathes in. The vocal cords are strongly vibrating, and the pitch, or melody, of the voice falls sharply with each pulse. The quality of the sound is similar to a 'mouth-wide-open' vowel such as [a]; hardly any features of a cry resemble later consonants, though you do often hear a hard 'catch' at the beginning or end of a pulse (technically known as a 'glottal stop'). Other qualities of sound may be present, too, such as a harsh, husky tone, quaintly known as 'vocal fry'.

Can different types of infant vocalization be distinguished? The hunger and pain cries tend to merge into a single distress cry, though some mothers have no difficulty telling the two apart. The pain cry may be much tenser, contain some very high pitches and pitch jumps, and have a different rhythm. The fussing sounds of discomfort are quite distinct, being only about ½ second long, and occurring in much shorter sequences. Vegetative noises, too, are very different from distress cries: they are briefer still (around ¼ of a second), and contain many more consonant-like sounds (such as the lips smacking together, or releasing a burst of [s]-like friction). Rare, abnormal cry-patterns also occur, in children suffering from brain damage or other severely handicapping physical conditions. Such cries are often very harsh or high-pitched, and lack the normal rhythm and pitch-movement of a healthy cry.

Is there anything we can learn about language development from these early cries? They'll tell us nothing about particular languages, of course, because these vocalizations are governed by biological factors, which are common to the whole human race. There's no such thing as an 'English birth cry' or a 'French hunger cry' or a 'German burp' – not at this age, at any rate. The point has even been checked out in a research study, by tape recording the cries of babies from several language backgrounds, and seeing whether people can tell them apart. They can't.

On the other hand, cries and other noises do share certain characteristics with later speech. Speech requires the active use of an outward flow of air from the lungs. So does crying. Speech requires the rhythmical stringing together of sounds over an extended period of time. So does crying. Speech requires the active use of the vocal cords in the production of vowels and some consonants. Vowel-like sounds are the mainstay of crying. Speech involves the use of pitch movements to express our feelings. Crying uses pitch movement too. Speech requires the movement of the vocal organs to produce different types of consonant sound. This can be observed in the production of the vegetative noises, and even occasionally in crying.

The child won't see it like this, nor will the parent: but it must be the case that while babies cry, root, and gurgle, they are getting practice in moving their vocal organs and controlling the flow of air through mouth and nose. It is only a small step along the long road to spoken language, but it is a fundamental one.

Stage 2 (8–20 weeks): cooing and laughing

Between 6 and 8 weeks, babies begin to make the sounds generally known as 'cooing'. They are produced when the baby is in a settled state, and are often thought of as comfort noises. Cooing sounds don't grow out of crying; rather, they develop alongside crying, gradually becoming more frequent and varied. They are sometimes heard as early as the first few days of life, but they don't become a major part of the child's output until after 2 months. At that time they usually emerge in response to the mother, when she smiles and talks to the baby. And the mother's speech quickly tunes in to these new sounds: as we shall see (p. 51), she is at the cooing stage too!

The sounds are certainly very different from anything else produced so far. They are quieter, lower-pitched, more musical. At the beginning of this period, each segment of cooing is quite short (about ½ second). It consists of a short vowel-like sound, usually preceded by a consonant-like sound made towards the back of the mouth, where the tongue and palate approach each other. Many of the sounds have a very nasal quality, because the mouth is not widely open, and air is passing out through the nose.

There's a great deal of variation in the types of sound made. Sounds resembling [g] and [k] are common, as are the several friction sounds which can be made in the same part of the mouth. You can sometimes hear a *ch* sound, which will remind you of the ending of such Scottish words as *loch*, or a uvular [r] sound similar to the one often used in French or German. Several types of vowel-like sound can also be heard, especially those made in the centre or at the back of the mouth – some resemble [u], others are more like the final sound of such words as *sofa* or *butter*. Put these sounds together and you get such sequences as [kuu] or [guu]. It's easy to see where the word 'cooing' comes from!

Later in this period, babies start stringing cooing sounds together – sometimes as many as 10 or 12 at a time. This is nothing like connected speech, though. The segments are usually separated by a short intake of breath, the rhythm is very erratic, and there is no melodic 'shape' to the sequence, as would be heard in a real sentence. On the other hand, it is possible to hear groups of sounds which at times are remarkably like the syllables of later speech, such as [ga] and [gu]. And the vowel-like sounds become yet more varied, some even taking on the character of a diphthong (a two-part vowel, such as [au] or [ou]). At 4–5 months, some children can coo very 'fluently' indeed.

From around 3 months, the vegetative sounds of the early weeks begin to die away, and the amount of crying becomes much less. Soon, most of the child's vocal day is taken up with cooing sounds. And then, at around 4 months, the first throaty chuckles and laughs emerge. For many parents, that is the first convincing sign that they have a social human being on their hands, not just an automatic food-processor.

The cooing stage is an important step forward towards spoken language. It's a stage when the baby begins to develop a greater measure of control over the muscles of the vocal organs. Over 100 sets of muscles are involved in the production of the vowels and consonants of speech, and it takes a great deal of practice to ensure that each set works in the right place at the right time. In cooing, we see the first gross steps in that direction. The tongue starts being moved upwards and downwards, forwards and backwards, just as will one day be required for speech. The vocal cords vibrate along with these tongue movements, in an increasingly precise sequence: sometimes, they vibrate throughout the whole of a cooing segment, as with [ga]; sometimes, they start vibrating halfway through, as with [ka]. This is a major step forward. When children have learned to coordinate their vocal cord movements with their tongue movements, they are well on their way to speech.

One other curious behaviour should be noted, at this stage. Often these children make their lips move, and their tongue push against them, almost as if they were trying to form more complex sounds – but few sounds in fact emerge. Parents often notice this behaviour, and think of it as an attempt at talking. 'What are you trying to tell me?' said one mother to her baby who was busily engaged in tongue-thrusting and lip-groping. 'You *are* saying a lot today', said another. Why babies do this isn't entirely clear, but they are probably copying the lip movements of the parents. Certainly, we know that young children are very ready to imitate: in one study, babies as young as 1 month were seen to imitate adults who stuck their tongue out at them. For all we know, babies at the cooing stage may be the youngest lip-readers alive.

Stage 3 (20–30 weeks): vocal play

Between 16 and 20 weeks of age, cooing sounds begin to die away. They are replaced by sounds which are much more definite and controlled. Cooing sounds often have a very shaky, uncertain quality; the sounds of vocal play, by contrast, are much steadier and longer (most take over 1 second). Each segment of vocal play consists of a single vowel-like or consonant-like sound, which is pronounced over and over. This is what gives the stage its name: the baby seems to take great pleasure in such repetitions.

The sounds are produced at a high pitch level, and wide glides of pitch from high to low are very noticeable. The vowel-like sounds are now much more varied than they were at stage 2. So are the consonant-like sounds. In particular, you'll be able to hear several sounds made at the front of the mouth – nasal sounds such as [mmm] and [nnn], or friction sounds such as [fff]. The tongue may make contact with the lips, to produce some very bubbly noises. Some of these friction noises are produced with great force. If the lips are kept tense, they may start to vibrate: the result is a 'trilled' sound which, in older children, would be considered extremely rude! Babies seem to take a perverse delight in producing long sequences of 'raspberries' at this age.

No one has yet been able to work out an order of appearance for the many sounds that are heard in vocal play. Some babies seem to begin by making sounds at the back of the mouth and then change to making them at the front. Others do exactly the opposite. Some spend several days, or even weeks, producing sequences of high and low pitch glides; then suddenly they switch to a different type of sound. Others alternate much more often. Most of the variation in vowel-like sounds, however, doesn't emerge until towards the end of this period. Also, at around 6–7 months, some of these sounds begin to combine into longer sequences. A vowel-like sound may be followed by a strong piece of lip friction, or an [mmm] may be followed by a vowel. Sometimes, syllables such as [ba] or [ta] can be heard, though the consonant sounds are not very precisely formed. One day, two or three such syllables are heard together. This is the first sign of the emergence of babbling.

What does the baby get out of this stage? There's plainly a lot of fun to be had, as can be seen from the way mother and baby spend long periods happily imitating each other. I have heard a two minute conversation which consisted entirely of raspberries on both sides! On the other hand, 'play' is a misleading label for the stage, because it doesn't convey the other thing that the baby is doing: getting *practice*, at a very important time. At this age, the proportions of the baby's head and neck are rapidly growing, and the vocal organs are moving into positions which are much more like those of an adult. The tongue has more room to move, and fresh places to move to. There is thus a great deal of oral pioneering work to be done: new positions for the tongue to explore, and new sounds to make. At the same time, the baby experiments with the different speeds at which the vocal cords can vibrate. Make them vibrate very fast, and the pitch of my voice goes high! Make them vibrate slowly, and my pitch is low! And if I'm *very* clever, I can get all the way from high to low in one long glide! There's a great deal going on, in all parts of the mouth and throat. Practice hasn't made perfect at the end of this stage, but it has made progress, and promoted a great deal of pleasure along the way.

Stage 4 (25–50 weeks): babbling

Babbling is the most familiar of all the types of sound a baby makes in the first year of life. Everyone knows of the typical [abababababa] or [dadadada] sequences which emerge from around 6 months. Technically, this kind of babbling is known as 're-duplicated' babbling, because the consonant-like sound is the same in every syllable.

Babbling is very different from the sounds of vocal play. In particular, it is much less varied, especially in the early part of the period. From a stage when the baby is experimenting with different kinds of sound in all parts of the mouth, we find a stage when a very small number of sounds are used – but with much greater frequency and stability.

About halfway through this period (around 9 months),

though, a different form of babbling arises which moves away from these fixed patterns. The consonants and vowels begin to change from one syllable to the next. You'll hear such sequences as [adu] and [maba]. A much wider range of sounds begins to be used, including many of the more complex friction sounds used in later speech (such as [s] and [ʃ] – the first sound of *shoe*). The rhythm of babbled sounds, and the length of the syllables, is much closer now to that which will soon be used for speech. This development is known as 'variegated' babbling.

What is going on in babbling? The utterances don't seem to have any meaning, though adults do sometimes play games with a baby's babble – imitating it, and trying to elicit more of it. They also hear 'words' in it, and try to persuade the baby to speak. An English mother, for example, may think her baby has named her when she hears [mamamama]; but, alas, this is not so. The real word for *mummy* will not appear for some while yet. Children mean nothing by these sequences, no matter how like the language they sound. On the other hand, during this period, they do begin to use other forms of communication in a meaningful way – gestures, such as pointing, are particularly common.

How does babbling relate to spoken language? It used to be thought that there was no link at all. During the babbling period the child was thought to try out every possible sound, in all the languages of the world, in a purely random way. In this view, the sounds of babbling have nothing to do with the later sounds of speech. When one stops, the other starts – sometimes separated by a period of silence, on the part of the child.

Several detailed studies of the sounds of babbling have shown that this theory does not hold. There are certainly some random sounds – including some which are never used in human languages – but the vast majority consist of a fairly small set of sounds, very similar to the sounds used in the early language to be spoken by the child. Some consonants are much more common than others. In three large American surveys, [h] and [d] came out top each time. [b], [m], [g], [w] and [j] were strongly represented too. But sounds such as [r], [f] and [z] were hardly found at all.

It isn't possible to say anything definite about the order in which the sounds of babbling emerge: there seem to be lots of individual differences among the children. Also, when you listen to babble, it isn't always easy to be sure which sound a baby is making, because its tongue and lip movements are not always precise. But there are certainly several similarities between the patterns of babbling and those of early spoken language. Early speech avoids clusters of consonants (such as [sp] or [tr]); so does babbling. Early speech prefers consonants to occur before vowels rather than after ([ta] rather than [at], for instance); so does babbling. Early speech replaces friction sounds by 'stopped' sounds at the beginnings of words (*see* might be pronounced [ti], for instance); so does babbling. Several other similarities have been noted.

If babbling and early speech have so much in common, might it be that the one shades into the other? Does speech start where babbling leaves off? This can't be so, because there are many cases on record of children continuing to babble long after they have begun to speak! It isn't at all odd for a child to be 'bilingual' in this way – developing a good spoken vocabulary on the one hand, and jabbering away in an unintelligible jargon on the other. Children as old as 18 months have still been heard to use vari-egated babble, in a very rhythmical and melodic way. It sounds like normal conversation except it is totally uninterpretable.

Nor is there much evidence to support the idea that the sounds of babbling gradually 'drift' towards the sounds of speech, a drift which becomes more marked as the babbling period proceeds. Some children show signs of this happening, but most don't. After all, if there were a noticeable drift, it would mean that English children, after a while, would have a marked English 'colouring' to their babble, which would be different from the babbling sounds of French, Chinese, and other children. Does this happen? If we had an English, French, and Chinese child in front of us, all babbling away, would we be able to tell them apart? The few studies which have been done suggest that the answer is no, though the results are somewhat mixed and this conclusion is not accepted by everyone.

The similarities between the sounds of late babbling and those of early speech are striking, though, and not just in English, but in many languages. Japanese, Hindi, Arabic, German, and other children all prefer the same kinds of consonants (such as nasals, and the stops), and avoid others (such as the friction sounds). The brain is obviously controlling the development of babbling and of early speech in a very similar way. But the two processes are separate. As a result of babbling, the child has a set of well-practised sounds which are tailor-made for speech. All that's needed is for them to be put to use for communicating meaning. During the babbling period, the child 'gets its act together', but it has yet to learn what the act is for.

Babbling is sometimes said to be a way of practising the sounds and sequences which will later be used in speech, without the child having to worry about the meaning of what's being uttered. There's some truth in this, and a good babbler is likely to be a good talker. But this doesn't always follow. Children suffering from Down's syndrome babble well, and in a similar way to normal children, but their subsequent spoken language development is often very poor. And there have been some very quiet babies, whose subsequent language development has been excellent.

No one has yet discovered a simple link between babbling and speech, and you should view all claims to 'explain' babble with great suspicion. For instance, frequent and varied babbling has been said to be a sign of good hearing, because the child listens to its sounds, likes what it hears, and produces more of them. This isn't so. The babbling of deaf children is very similar to that of hearing children. Similarly, claims about memory, intelligence, personality, and other psychological attributes have been much exaggerated. We just don't know whether children who babble a lot tend to have extrovert personalities, or be more intelligent. But one thing we do know: it ain't *necessarily* so.

Stage 5 (9 months–18 months): melodic utterance

Towards the end of the first year, the baby's utterances become much more varied. A wider range of sounds enters the babbling, as we've seen. And, from around 9 months, the melody, rhythm, and tone of voice of the utterances develop also. These are the features which make language sound fluent and natural, and some children become very adept at manipulating them. We've already noted the way in which long strings of babbled sounds can be built up, sounding like a perfectly normal conversation, apart from the absence of any meaning. This 'expressive jargon', or 'scribble talk', is especially common after 12 months.

But to begin with, the patterns of melody and rhythm are much less frequent and definite. They begin to emerge between 6 and 9 months. For the most part, the babble rambles on in its erratic, jerky way: sometimes loud, sometimes soft; sometimes fast, sometimes slow; sometimes high, sometimes low. Then, quite suddenly, a 'chunk' of babble stands out, with a more definite shape. It gives you a clear impression that the baby is trying to say something. It's impossible to say what, but parents quickly feel that their child is trying to be more communicative. They say things like 'He's definitely trying to tell us something', and they associate different melodies with different situations. 'She's asking for her panda again', 'I think he wants to go back in his bouncer.'

As time goes by, parents hazard more definite interpretations – the utterances sound as if they're questioning, exclaiming, labelling, calling, greeting ... Several fixed melodies develop, too, as the child picks them up from the various games and rituals played by the parents. For instance, at the end of each meal, parents often say *all gone*, with a sing-song, high-low melody. I recorded one child who had picked this phrase up enthusiastically: he would take great delight from saying it *before* his mother did. He didn't do very well with the consonants and vowels, but he produced the phrase with a perfect melody and rhythm. Another child 'asked' his mother to play the game 'round-and-round-the-garden': the utterance had a confused mix of sounds, none of which sounded much like the name of the game but the rhythm was quite clearly 'tum-ti-tum-ti-*tum*-ti', and the final *tum* had a lovely gliding rise in pitch, just as the mother said when she played it.

These melodies and rhythms are the first signs of real language development in children. Children from different language backgrounds now begin to sound increasingly unlike each other. An English child's utterances consist of a 'tum-ti-tum' rhythm, which contrasts with that of a French child; this, in turn, displays more of the 'rat-tat-tat' rhythm characteristic of French speech. A Chinese child begins to sound more 'sing-song'. And deaf children, at this stage, come to sound increasingly abnormal, for their speech lacks the expected range of these melodic and rhythmical variations.

Then, at around 12 months, we hear the final episode in the pre-speech saga. Short utterances, just one or two syllables long, with a clear melody and rhythm, come to be made in a regular and predictable way. [daa], said Jamie, with a rising melody, one day; and the next day, he said it several dozen times; and the next day, several hundred. No one was quite sure what it meant to begin with. It sounded as if he was trying to say *that*, but this interpretation didn't always fit the situation. It made sense when he said it while pointing at a passing cat. His mother immediately said 'What's that? That's a pussy cat'. But it didn't seem to make sense when he said it in an off-the-cuff way over his mother's shoulder as he was being whisked off to bed. And everyone ignored it. Was it a word, or wasn't it? Some people have invented the term 'proto-word' for this kind of thing. In the transition from pre-language to language, children often produce many of these proto-words, where the sounds are clear, but the meaning isn't. Only when the sound of an utterance and its meaning *both* become clear do we have the final step: a 'first word'.

Perceiving and understanding

We've seen that there's a lot of sound-making that goes on before the appearance of the first word. But there's an even greater amount of sound-receiving. In fact, this is one of the clearest reasons why we can't say that language begins at around age 1. The *production* of spoken language begins about then; but the *comprehension* of spoken language starts well before this.

How far back do we have to go? When do children first start to understand the speech that adults direct at them? More basically, when do they first start to *perceive* it? There's an important difference between perception and comprehension, as anyone knows who's been in contact with a foreign language. It's easy enough to perceive that foreigners are talking to you; but working out what they're saying is a very different matter. And a similar problem must face the baby during the first year.

How far back, then? The amazing answer to this question is: all the way. Right back to birth, and perhaps even before.

Psychologists have been able to show all kinds of auditory abilities in the new-born baby. Babies turn their heads towards the source of a sound within the first few days. They prefer human voices to non-human sounds as early as 2 weeks. They can even recognize their mother's voice before they are a day old. How do we know? By carrying out experiments in which we play different sounds to the baby, and carefully monitor the responses it makes. In one experiment, for instance, day-old babies heard the mother's voice speaking normally, the mother's voice speaking abnormally (in a monotone), and a stranger's voice. Only the first caused the babies to attend.

Of course, what isn't clear is whether babies learn this feat of recognition in the first 24 hours, or whether they can do it already. Perhaps they learn to identify their mother's voice while still within the womb. It wouldn't be very surprising if they did. We know that the structures of the ear are fully formed within 5 months of conception. The tiny bones in the middle ear (the ossicles), for example, are as they will be in the adult (they are the only bones which do not grow after birth). The nerve which leads from the ear to the brain is already sheathed in the tissue (myelin) which makes it capable of transmitting nerve impulses efficiently, whereas many other nerves at birth have yet to develop this covering. It is as if the human being is programmed with the ability to hear.

Moreover, there is plenty to hear within the womb. The flow of blood, the process of digestion, the passage of fluids and other movements make the womb an extremely noisy environment. To hear anything against this background cannot be easy and yet it is possible to show that the baby responds to sounds played to it. It must be able to 'pay attention' to sound, therefore, something which is crucial if spoken language skills are to develop. And with four months to go, and nothing much else to do, it's perhaps reasonable to think of the new-born baby as someone with a whole range of expectations about the nature of sound, and some ability to focus on patterns of sound that are of particular significance – such as the mother's voice.

But what about the individual sounds of speech? Can babies hear these early on, and tell the difference between them? Could a new-born baby hear the distinction between [pa] and [ba], for example? An enormous amount of research has been devoted to such questions, and the answers are hotly debated. But on the whole, people agree that infants from around 4 weeks of age can tell the difference between several pairs of consonants or vowels which are used in the adult language around them, such as [p] and [b], or [a] and [i]. Some differences in melody and rhythm can also be distinguished at this age. The infants don't discriminate all sounds with equal efficiency, and there are clear signs of development as they grow: in one study, for example, [s] and [z] were not distinguished until around 6 months. But a basic perceptual ability seems to be present from a very early age. Some, indeed, think it may be present at birth.

The problem, of course, is to devise ways of finding out about these things. How do the psychologists *know* that a 1-month-old can discriminate consonants? The usual method is to play sounds to the child through a pair of headphones, or a loudspeaker, while monitoring the baby's responses – such as the speed of its heartbeat, or the speed at which it sucks on a nipple. In the second approach, for instance, the baby is given a special nipple which contains an instrument that measures its rate of sucking. Then a particular sound is played over and over to it. As it gets used to the sound, the speed of sucking settles down to a particular rate. Next, a different sound is played to the child. If it notices the difference, the rate of sucking will suddenly increase, and then slow down again.

Of course, there's a big jump between showing that babies can discriminate single sounds in simple syllables, such as [pa] versus [ba], and showing that the same abilities operate when these sounds are used in the stream of speech, by different speakers, in different settings, to express different meanings. Also, it is sometimes quite difficult deciding when there has been a clear response, on the baby's part. But after allowing for these problems, we are still left with a definite indication that speech perception skills develop very early indeed.

When does perception become comprehension? The first signs of real understanding arise when babies begin to respond to the different tones of voice adults use, usually between 2 and 4 months. Several contrasts in meaning come to be appreciated – the difference between angry, soothing, and playful voices, for instance. By between 6 and 9 months, the child can recognize the different use of certain utterances in their situations. 'Time for tea' might make the baby turn towards the high-chair; 'Let's find daddy', towards the door. 'Say bye-bye' might produce a wave; 'clap hands', a clap. Some types of questions begin to be understood. One 10-month-old child liked to play 'where' games with his mother ('Where's teddy?', 'Where's pussycat?', and so on); in most cases he would turn or point to the object correctly.

Above all, individual words may also be recognized, especially if they occur often, and have a very clear meaning – such as *no*, *ta*, the child's own name, or the name of the family dog. Well before the end of the first year, in fact, most children have built up a small vocabulary of words whose meaning they understand quite well. In one study of eight children, six showed clear evidence of understanding up to 20 words before the end of the first year, and one child understood as many as 60. In all cases, though, the ability to produce words lagged behind the ability to comprehend by at least a month. There may not have been 'first words' present in these children, but there were certainly 'first meanings'.

Talking together

It's usual to think of conversation as something which takes place between two people who both speak the same language. If you don't speak French, you can't have a conversation with a French person who doesn't speak English. This simple principle works well enough for talk between adults; but it doesn't work at all for talk between adults and babies in the first year. Here's a conversation with a 3-month-old, to illustrate the point. It looks very one-sided, but there were definitely two participants, who took it in turns to talk. Unfortunately, one party's contribution to the conversation consisted solely of cries, gurgles, splutters, and cooing sounds, to which it isn't possible to do justice, using the letters of the alphabet.

Michael: (*loud crying*)
Mother: Oh my word, what a noise! What a noise! (*picks up Michael*)
Michael: (*sobs*)

Mother: Oh dear, dear, dear. Didn't anybody come to see you? Let's have a look at you (*looks inside nappy*). No, you're all right there, aren't you.

Michael: (*spluttering noises*)

Mother: Well, what is it, then? Are you hungry, is that it? Is it a long time since dinner-time?

Michael: (*gurgles and smiles*)

Mother (*nuzzles baby*): Oh yes it is, a long long time.

Michael: (*cooing noise*)

Mother: Yes, I know. Let's go and get some lovely grub, then. How about that . . .

and so on, and so on, for several minutes more.

No other form of human interaction displays anything quite like this. Moreover, it's been going on from the first day of the baby's life. As soon as a baby is born, mothers hold it in front of them and talk to it. It's the most natural thing in the world – and one of the oddest things, too, to talk at such length to someone who doesn't understand your language.

But of course the whole point, which most mothers instinctively grasp, is to get real communication going as soon as possible. Almost everything the mother says, in the first few months of life, is controlled by what the baby does, and the noises it makes. The child can't lift a finger without mother giving it a meaning. Even yawns, burps, sneezes, and other biological noises are interpreted as if they were messages of the greatest significance. Things stay this way for several months.

Surprising as it may seem, the result is highly satisfying for all concerned. Baby makes a noise, so mother makes a noise in return. Baby makes a different noise and mother makes a different noise back. At the same time, she introduces all kinds of extra melodies, rhythms, and tones of voice into her speech to see what produces the best reactions. And the baby responds accordingly. There's satisfaction and enjoyment all round. A foundation for social interaction has been laid. There may be no child language yet, but there's lots of communication.

Things develop very quickly. At around 5 weeks, the exchanges become more emotional, and there's a great deal of mutual smiling. As the baby's utterances change, so the mother's change too. At around 8 weeks, the baby begins to coo, and the mother's speech becomes softer and gentler. A month or so later, the child starts to look around, and the mother speaks more loudly, as she tries to draw the child's attention to different objects. Her speech melody becomes more exaggerated, and she often repeats her sentences. The baby starts to laugh, and this is the greatest encouragement of all. The mother's voice becomes more varied, and this in turn encourages the baby to make more noises.

Communication becomes even more successful when, around this time, parents start playing simple games with the baby. Face-to-face play, such as peekaboo, is especially appreciated, as are games with parts of the body such as 'Round-and-round-the-garden' and 'This little piggy went to market'. By around 6 months, the games become more sophisticated. Some are 'sound games', as parents imitate their child, who in turn imitates them. Others involve the use of objects, and baby's role begins to resemble that of a sports commentator. You don't just throw something on the floor for someone else to pick up: you make a great deal of noise while doing so!

Shortly after 6 months, things change yet again. Babies are now sitting up, and making more purposeful movements. They are exploring more, with hands and (especially) mouths. The mother's utterances change, as a consequence. She no longer talks just of the child, but begins to speak in a routine way about other objects and actions. 'That's horrid', said one mother, referring to the baby's attempt to sink his gums into a tennis ball, and this led to a one-minute dissertation on the function of tennis balls and where they should be kept – to which the baby listened, rapt.

Between 8 and 10 months, babies are able to attract the attention of others by pointing, and this further moves the focus away from themselves and towards the objects and events of the outside world. They can be seen now to 'follow' adult conversations, looking first at one person, then at the other. Their shouts for attention become increasingly insistent and unmistakable. Their comments about world affairs become more deliberate and provocative, especially as 12 months approaches. Adults who try to carry on a conversation across a child of this age do so at their peril.

The whole of this first year provides children with an ideal language learning environment. They find themselves in contact with native speakers of the language who are on hand 24 hours a day, who respond to their every noise, and continually talk to them in short, simple, repetitive sentences. And, as the year goes by, these people do their best to ensure that language learning is fun, by providing all kinds of stimulating games. The games provide lots of practice in learning words and phrases, because the same game is played over and over. Many of them improve the ability to take turns with others, an essential feature of all conversation. And all of them make the baby observe carefully what the other person is doing and saying: you have to pay attention. No foreign language learner ever gets such treatment, or could ever afford such treatment!

Above all, the baby learns from a game that it doesn't take much to communicate – a point which has been well made by Jerome Bruner, who illustrates it from the 'bouncing games' which often take place while parents recite a nursery rhyme. If you bounce a child on your knee in time to 'The grand old Duke of York', or 'Ride a cock horse', it's very natural to give the child an especially large bounce when you get to the last line. When the child gets used to this, it's just as natural to pause before this last line, making the child 'wait for it'. The baby will wriggle or vocalize expectantly, and this provides a signal that they want the game to carry on. You finish off the game, and their expectation is fulfilled. There can't be an easier or more enjoyable way of learning what communication is all about.

To conclude

By the end of the first year, as children approach their 'first words', a great deal of preliminary linguistic spadework has already taken place. They have learned a great deal about how to pronounce and listen to sounds; they have made inroads into the comprehension of the language used around them; and they have begun to learn the basis of all social interaction – how to carry on a conversation. The next step is to put all of this learning to work, in the active use of the sounds, grammar, and vocabulary of their language. The language now has its foundations, and it needs a first floor. This will be built in the second year of life.

Feature 2 | Fathers and mothers

If all goes well, children come to learn several basic conversational skills by 12 months of age. This is largely due to the way mothers develop their own special way of talking, to get the most out of their children – a style which is usually called 'motherese'. It's sometimes referred to as 'baby talk', but this is a rather misleading label because many people think of baby talk as the use of childish words, such as *moo-cow*, and there's far more to motherese than that. Apart from using simple vocabulary, mothers alter a large part of their grammar and pronunciation. They come to speak more slowly than usual, and they widen the pitch of their voice. Their sentences become shorter and simpler; and they repeat utterances several times.

'Fatherese' is not very different. Fathers also change their voices and simplify their sentences. Several studies have counted the kinds of utterance that mothers use, and those that fathers use, and got virtually the same results for each. On the other hand, it wouldn't be surprising to find *some* differences between mothers' and fathers' speech to their children. After all, in most family situations fathers are not around as much. Mothers have many times more opportunity to talk to their baby, especially in the early months, though new patterns of (un)-employment are already changing this situation. They've therefore had more practice in adapting their speech to the child's needs.

It turns out that there are a few differences, and they might be quite important. Mothers are much more likely to chat when they're with their baby. Fathers, however, are much less likely to understand the baby's vocalizations. They use a wider range of vocabulary, when they talk to the baby; and they ask more direct questions, especially when playing with older children. Also, although fathers have less time to be with the baby, when they do get round to interacting, they do so in a much more intense way – playing more dramatically, or bouncing more dangerously.

Mothers often don't know whether to be scared or delighted when they see such things go on!

Because of these differences, it's often thought that mother and father unconsciously take on complementary roles, when they talk to their children. The mother's role is to support the child as much as possible. The father's is to place more demands on the child, and to make fewer allowances for problems of communication. By being less sensitive to the child's needs, it is argued, he acts as a kind of bridge between the home and the cruel outside world, which won't make so many linguistic allowances either. It's a nice idea but it probably doesn't provide the whole explanation, especially these days when social attitudes to male and female roles are changing. 'Parentese' is one of those research fields which, along with the baby, is in its infancy.

Feature 3 | **Mama and dada**

Everyone knows that most children spend more time with their mothers than with their fathers, in the first year or so of life. So it may come as a surprise to learn that most children use the word for 'father' earlier and much more often than the word for 'mother'. Here are some recorded cases:

– a Slovenian child studied in 1959 referred to his father (*ata*) at 0;6.27, but his mother (*mama*) wasn't referred to until nearly a year later – 1;5.7;

– a Czech child studied in 1958 referred to his father (*tata*) at 1;0, and to his mother (*mama*) nearly two months later (1;1.25);

– an American English child studied in 1984 (see p. 95) said *daddy* about two months before *mommy* (= British English *mummy*); on the other hand, the two other children in the same study produced the two words at almost the same time, with *mommy* slightly ahead;

– another English child studied in 1975 tried to say *daddy* seven times at 0;11, but made no reference to his mother until about a month later; throughout the whole study, *daddy* was used more than twice as often as *mama*.

One study took the form of an experiment. The researchers showed children slides of their mother, their father, and other male and female adults, and noted what they said when they saw the picture come up on the screen. It turned out that they were far more likely to say *daddy* when they were shown a slide of their father than they were to say *mummy* when shown a slide of their mother.

Why should this be? Do the children take their mothers more for granted? Do they identify more with one than the other? Are fathers more like objects who have to be given a separate 'label'? A much simpler explanation was proposed by John Locke in a 1985 report.

We know from the studies of babbling that some sounds are more likely to be used by a child than others; and that when children start to talk, they show similar preferences (p. 43). There are also some studies which show that young children are more likely to attempt to say words which contain these 'favourite' sounds, and learn them more quickly than words which don't have these sounds. Adults often feel the same way about the words in a foreign language: it's much easier to use and remember words if they're easy to pronounce, and words which contain difficult sounds are often avoided. Could this explain why *daddy*, with its repeated [d] sounds is preferred to *mummy*, with its repeated [m] sounds?

It seems very likely. Three big American surveys of the sounds used by English-speaking babies at around 1 year of age all came up with the same results. On average, children at this age are *five* times more likely to be using sounds such as [t] and [d] than sounds such as [m]. Words like *daddy* are going to be much easier to say, therefore, than words like *mummy*.

There are exceptions, of course: in one study, the child had five times as many *mama*s as *dada*s! But that child had a preference for babbling [m] sounds, and found [d] sounds generally difficult. So she may not have been an exception after all. She ended up giving priority to the word whose sounds she used most when babbling.

These biases aren't unique to English. The babbling preferences have been found in several languages. And the preference for 'father' words to have a [t] or a [d], and for 'mother' words to have a nasal sound, is also very widespread.

Which leaves the $64,000 question. Why have words for 'father', over the course of human history, come to be more pronounceable than words for 'mother'? Answers on a postcard, please.

Who are all these wonderful mothers and fathers who talk to their children so well and get the most out of them (I hear you say)? Are normal people like that?

Well, yes, actually. When researchers study parent–child interaction, they don't check out on the family first, and choose only those who are likely to be 'good' mothers and fathers. How on earth could anyone say, especially when it's the first child? The selection is always made much more randomly – asking for volunteers through an advertisement, or even using a pin to pick names out of a list (such as a voting roll, or a telephone directory). In other words, anyone could be approached. The parents who have cooperated in these studies are normal, everyday parents, rather tickled that someone should be interested in their children. The only obvious bias is that they have usually been people of middle-class backgrounds, and, so far, most of the studies have been made of white children. Apart from this, there's no reason to think that the findings wouldn't apply generally.

But on the other hand, it's a fact of life that not everyone finds it equally easy to talk to babies. Indeed, some people find it difficult talking to *anyone*, whatever their age. So what do you do if you're a naturally quiet parent, and you don't find your linguistic instincts working as well as the research suggests they should?

The short answer is that you may have to go out of your way to provide your child with the stimulation it needs. The research makes it quite clear that the only way to a good command of language is to feed the child language from the outset. I choose the metaphor of 'feeding' deliberately, rather than, say, 'bathing'. People sometimes talk about 'bathing the child in language', but this isn't the way to think about it. The equivalent of bathing would be simply to plonk the child down in front of the television. But this won't work. Speech is an active skill. The development of pronunciation, the turn-taking, and all the other things which go on in the first year cannot take place just by sitting back, enjoying the pictures and sucking on a rusk. Natural language learn-ing takes place in an environment of excitement and fun. It takes two to talk. And the talking has to be *to* each other, not *at*. Spoken language has to be directed towards the child, if it is to be effective.

So – to continue the feeding metaphor – you may not eat very much yourself, but you'd be unwise to treat your child in the same way. You need to give the child the linguistic equivalent of a regular four-course meal, during the first year. What might this be?

You have to use the situations from which speech can naturally arise, in the course of every day, and which will promote *joint* activities. Here are a few such guidelines.

● Give the baby the chance to pay attention. If there's too much noise going on – and especially if the noise pattern is always changing (such as people coming in and out, or machines switching off and on)'– this will be difficult. If the radio is al-ways on, make sure it's turned off at the times when you decide to have a go at communicating with the baby. Always try to have some time alone with the child each day.

● 'Talking to' means 'looking at'. 'Look at me when I'm talking to you', Eric Morecambe used to say to Ernie Wise. To get real communication going with the baby, you have to keep in eye contact. This isn't too difficult when there's only you and the baby in the room, but when there are lots of others clamouring for your attention it can be a problem. Trying to feed the baby with one hand and keeping order with the other may be a regular family situation, but it does nothing for the baby's emerging language. Imagine how you'd feel if every time someone said something to you, and you tried to reply, they turned away to talk to someone else!

Does this mean that later-born children are always going to be delayed in their acquisition of language? Not at all, if you take care, and devote some time each day to baby talk without others interfering. The baby may not be getting as much language from you as the eldest brother or sister did a few years before (after all, some of your daily talk has to be devoted to *them*!), but perhaps that does not matter in the long run. After all, some of the directed talk which the baby needs can be provided by your allies, the

other brothers and sisters. In fact, often they are better at talking
to and understanding a baby than the parents are!

The same point applies to anyone else who is in regular contact
with the baby – grandparents, baby-minders, and so on. Once the
baby is used to them, they can all help to provide the right kind of
language environment. But strangers won't do. A new face
brimming with language will only put off a young child.
Grandparents who are occasional visitors have to understand
this, too. It takes time for the child to get used to a new voice, as
well as a new face. Often, words spoken by the 'stranger' won't be
understood.

Mother: Mike knows the dog's name, now. Look. Mike,
    where's Tom? Where's Tom?
Baby (10 months): (*points and makes a grunt*)
Mother: That's right. There he is. Good boy.
Visiting grandma: Clever boy. Where's Tom, Mike? Show me.
    Where's Tom?
Baby: (*looks away and fusses*)

Grandmas get disgruntled at this point, but they needn't be if they
realize the basic principle. You need familiarity before you breed
linguistic content.

The topic of the conversation needs to be familiar as well. I've
heard parents complaining bitterly about the political situation as
they change a baby. I remember one mother concluding 'So *you*
won't vote for Mrs Thatcher when you grow up, will you!' to her
6-month-old. There's no harm in this, of course, unless you get
carried away, and the baby gets frightened by your cross tone of
voice, but it can't possibly be as useful as a conversation which
the child might be expected to know something about.

What does the child know best? The rituals of every day –
feeding, changing, bathing and the like. These are just right for
language learning because the same words and phrases come up
again and again. One thing you can do is keep up a running
commentary while you perform the necessary actions. As you
move from washing one part of the body to the next, you can
name the different body-parts, and say what you're doing to them.
If the baby causes a splash, talk about the splash. If some water

goes in the eyes, talk about this fresh emergency. Ask lots of questions (*You're all wet, aren't you?*), and leave time for a 'reply'. Use lots of names for things (nouns). Above all, use as many words for actions as you can (verbs). Verbs, as we'll see, play a particularly important role in later language development.

But don't *worry* about the 'grammar' of the language you use. I've heard parents agonize over whether they might be doing some harm by not speaking in complete sentences, or by using special baby-talk words, such as *moo-cow* or *choo-choo*. These fears have absolutely no foundation. There's only one principle which works: be natural. If you find yourself using baby-talk, and it comes naturally (as it does for most people), then fine. If you think baby-talk sounds silly, and you can't bear to use it, equally fine. Similarly, you'll find some children who naturally fall into the use of baby words, and others who studiously avoid them. ''Snot a choo-choo, 's a train', a 2-year-old sternly told me once.

● Similarly, don't correct the child's language, to make it conform to the kind of grammar used by Lord Macaulay, or that you half-remember being taught in school. This is a point more relevant for children in their second and third years, of course, but it might as well be mentioned now. There's a time and a place for correcting grammar, and it isn't the first three or four years of life (see p. 190). You're wasting your time, if you try. Children won't linguistically run before they can walk. If they come out with something which sounds like an 'error', from the adult's point of view, you can be sure it's there for a reason. Often, the error shows that the child is getting on with the task of language learning – as we've already seen with Susie's attempt to sort out irregular verbs (p. 13). In these cases, it's a sign of *good* language development, not bad. But always there's a risk if you draw attention to an error, and try to correct it: you'll only add to the confusion, and you may do harm to the child's confidence and self-esteem. Left alone, the child will correct it spontaneously, in due course.

So, if the child says *Me got car*, don't say back to him 'Listen, Ted, say "*I've* got a car"'. Be subtle. Say 'Yes, you have, haven't you. And look, I've got a car too'. In this way, you get the best of both worlds. You reply to the child's remark as a normal human being should – and you drop a hint, a second later, that there just might have been a better way of saying such a sentence. Sharp children pick these clues up, though it may take a while (months, perhaps) before they use the more advanced grammar for themselves. And in the field of language handicap, techniques of this kind are thought to be a very important means of improving a child's grammatical skills.

● Likewise, don't try to correct the child's pronunciation, at this age. The sounds of a language are learned according to certain principles, as we shall see (p. 82), and they won't be rushed. One of the worst things you can do is insist on the child pronouncing something 'correctly' before you give something. It happens. [da] said an 18-month-old, pointing at his toy dog. 'Say *dog*', said the parent, emphasizing the final [g]. [da] said the child again. 'Not until you say *doG*', insisted the parent. The exchange went on for quite some time, with a fairly predictable result: tears and sweat all round. This kind of thing won't work, it doesn't help – and, for someone who doesn't know any better, it's not fair. Far better simply to accept the child's version, and then demonstrate the correct form by casually saying the word yourself as you pass the object over.

● Maintain the 'commentary' principle (see above) whenever possible. Talk about what's going on, especially in the baby's field of vision. Don't talk so much about what *has* happened or what *will* happen. These tense forms are, literally, a waste of time. Conversations which begin 'What did you see in the garden today?' or 'Do you know what we're going to do this afternoon...' have really a very limited function. Keep the topics to the 'here and now'. And make the language as specific as possible, especially as the child approaches the end of the first year, when there's a special interest in the meanings of words. 'Look at that' isn't going to be as helpful then as 'Look at that car'.

● As a last resort, if you can't think of anything to say, get some ideas from others – in the form of a brightly coloured picture book. Even if the baby's only 2 or 3 months old, a lot can be gained by showing the pictures and talking about them – even asking questions about them, and providing the answers yourself. Questions are a very important means of developing a sense of communication: they are the clearest sign that it's someone else's turn to speak.

● Whatever the joint activity, in due course the baby will begin to make some noises at you. It's very important then to listen attentively to these noises, and to talk back. As we've seen, babies will learn to communicate only if people treat them as communicators right from the start. Show lots of interest in everything they 'say'. Parental listening is just as important as parental talking.

● Last, don't overdo things. Don't be talking all the time. Babies like some peace and quiet too!

3 | The Second Year

Around 12 months of age a child's first words begin to appear. That's an average age, of course. A few children have been heard to produce real, identifiable words from as early as eight or nine months. Others babble on until 18 months or so, without producing a single definite word. Some even lapse into silence in their second year, not taking off until they're nearly two. These children often miss out the 'first word' stage completely, and launch themselves into language with complete sentences. One of my own children was like this. If I hadn't known better, I'd have begun to be worried by the time she was 18 months. But no: a few months later, she was chattering away just like any other 2-year-old. No one has yet been able to explain why such delays take place.

Lord Macaulay is said to have been a very late talker. There's a story told about him that, when language finally emerged (around age 3), he was asked why his first words had come so late, to which he is supposed to have replied: 'Hitherto, nothing of sufficient significance has warranted my verbal attention.'

I don't believe it either.

How much do they say?

Once a child produces a first word, others quickly follow. Helen Benedict studied the rate at which eight children produced new words. One child, Elizabeth, had no spoken vocabulary at 1;3.9 (one year, three months, nine days). Twenty days later, she had 20 words. By 1;4.12 she had 30. And by 1;6, she had 50. The other children performed in more or less the same way. The average time it took the children to get from 10 to 50 words was 4.8 months – that is, about 10 new words a month. Five of the children reached the 50-word level by 18 months. The slowest, Karen, didn't reach that level until 1;10,

"Tell your mother it's the official Census Enumerator from the Office of Population Censuses and Surveys."

but then she didn't begin to talk until she was 1;6 anyway.

Even more impressive progress is seen when we look at the words children understand. Everyone understands far more words than they ever use. The 'active' spoken vocabulary of educated adults may be as little as 20–30,000 words; but their 'passive' vocabulary – that is, the words they understand, but don't actively use – may be three or four times larger. The same applies to children who display this difference from the very beginning of their vocabulary learning. Elizabeth couldn't *produce* 20 words until 1;3, but she was able to *understand* 20 words soon after 11 months. She managed 50 spoken words at 1;6, but this was a long time after she reached that target in her comprehension – halfway through her thirteenth month! Indeed, by the time she was 1;3, she was able to understand over 150 words.

Once again, she is quite typical. On average, the children understood 50 words before they were able to produce 10, and they didn't arrive at a corresponding number in their speech until 5 months later. They understood an average of 22 new words each month – over twice as many as they learned to speak. There is evidently quite a gap between production and comprehension of vocabulary at this age.

Putting all this in a nutshell: by 18 months, a child can speak about 50 words, but it can understand about 5 times as many. By age 2, spoken vocabulary exceeds 200 words, and comprehension has increased to –? Here, we have a difficulty. Deciding whether a child has understood a word is one of the thorniest problems facing anyone who studies children's language. There are all kinds of uncertainties, as the following anecdotes show.

– 'Where's your bowl?' says a mother to Jimmy, a high-chaired 15-month-old, and he obediently points to the dishful of food. Later, having washed up, she passes the child carrying the clean dish and she asks the question again. This time, Jimmy looks confused, and doesn't respond. Does he understand the word *bowl* or doesn't he? If he does, why doesn't he point correctly? If he doesn't, how do you explain the first reaction? Perhaps he thinks the word *bowl* means 'food' or 'dinner', so that when it's clean it can't be a bowl any more.

– 'It's jamas time' says a mother to 18-month-old Michael at bedtime. He trots off to a cupboard and pulls out his pyjamas.

Next day, doing the washing, she puts out a pile of clothes on the ironing board and asks 'Which are your jamas?' Michael has no idea. Does he understand the word *jamas* or doesn't he? Or perhaps he only understands the word in its 'proper place' – that is, when it's getting on towards bedtime.

Children present us with numerous problems of this type, during the second year. After age 2, these problems become much less, because the children have learned more about the world and can handle more complicated sentences, so they can 'explain themselves' better. But by then, of course, it becomes even more difficult to count the words they understand, because adults are now talking so much to them. And no one has yet worked out any precise figures for the learning of vocabulary past age 2. The figure is up in the thousands somewhere.

What do they talk about?

Young children talk mainly about what is going on around them – the 'here and now'. If you decide to keep a diary of their words, as they appear (see p. 223), you'll find that it's possible to group them into the different 'fields' of meaning that the children want to talk about. Fields such as these:

People These are mainly relatives – obviously, *mummy* or (in America) *mommy*, and the other forms of this word (such as *mum* and *mama*), and *daddy* (*dad*, *papa*, and so on). Then there are the other members of the immediate family, such as *grandad*, *grandma*, and the names of brothers and sisters. *Baby* (or *baba*) is often used too, usually referring to the speaker! And we mustn't forget the regular callers at the house, such as *milkman* and *postman*, though at this stage they may simply be known as *man* or (see below) *dada*.

Actions The words associated with the major 'moves' in a child's day are quickly picked up, especially the most routine activities. Thus we hear *bye-bye*, *hello* (*hi*, *hi-yo*, and so on), *night-night*, *upsy-daisy*, *down you lie*, *all gone*, and *fall down*. In fact, a very large number of words used by the young child involve, directly or indirectly, the notion of 'movement' – they refer either to the way things move, to the things that can be moved, or to the people who move them. Very early on, children learn some basic action words, such as *give*, *show*, *kiss*, *get* or *got*, *splash*, *eat*, *tickle*, *put*, *play*, *say*, *jump*, and *go(ne)*. They also pick up the main words which stop actions taking place: *no* and *don't*!

Food Some very important words here, from the child's point of view: for instance, *milk*, *juice* (or a more specific word, such as *orange*), *drink* (pronounced *dink*, of course, at this age), *cookie* (in America), or *biscuit* (in Britain, often pronounced [bik]). There may be words for fruit, too, such as *banana* (usually pronounced [nana]) and *apple*. And the occasions of eating may be named, such as *din-din* and *tea*.

Parts of the body The first words in this field are usually for parts of the face – such as *mouth*, *nose*, *eye(s)* and *ear*. Later, the limbs begin to be talked about, such as *hand* (or, of course, *handie(s)*), *finger*, *thumb*, and *toes*. Body functions, such as *wee-wee* and *pooh*, come to be identified.

Clothing This includes such words as *hat*, *nappy* (in Britain; *diaper* in America), *shoes*, *pyjamas* (usually *jamas*), and *coat*.

Animals A very popular field. Domestic animals are the commonest, but farm and wild animals are also found, picked up from picture books or TV programmes. Examples include *dog* (*doggie*), *cat* (*pussy*, *pussycat*, and the like), *bird(ie)*, *cow*, *horse* (*horsie*), *sheep*, and *lion*. The sounds the animals make can also become the words, or part of the words: *moo* or *moo-cow*, *baa* or *baalamb*, *woof* or *woof-woof*.

Vehicles Another popular field. *Car*, *truck* (especially in America), *boat*, and *train* are among the commonest words, along with their noises, such as *brmbrm* and *beep*. There's a big difference between town and country here, of course. The city dweller will be saying *bus* and *lorry* long before country cousin does. On the other hand, country cousin will be well ahead when it comes to *tractor*. I was once solemnly assured by a farmer's wife that the word [baam] issuing from the mouth of her 15-month-old scrap was 'combine harvester'!

Toys A lot of variation here, but *ball*, *brick(s)* or *block(s)*, *book*, and *doll(ie)* are usually among the earliest. Games such as *clap-hands* or *peep-bo* (*peekaboo*) are often given a name.

Household objects The important words here are all to do with the child's daily routine, such as *cup*, *spoon*, *bowl* or *plate*, *bottle*, *brush*, or *light*. Objects which make a noise are often singled out for special attention, such as *clock* (or *tick-tock*), *hoover* and *washing machine* (usually reduced to a single syllable, such as *'chine*).

Locations A few words are used to express the idea of an object's location – such as *where*, *where's*, *look*, *there*, *in* and *on*. These words are usually used while the child is searching for something, or putting something somewhere.

Social words The important words here are *yes* and *no*, and the words which signal politeness, such as *please* and *thank you* (or *ta*). Some parents stress these notions a lot in the second year, though it's more usual not to find them being emphasized until the third year. An important verb which relates to this field is *want*.

Describing words In later grammar, these are the words which we would call 'adjectives', such as *hot* (said of food, ovens, and the like), *nice*, *dirty*, *pretty*, and *big*. They become an increasingly important part of a young child's vocabulary.

'Empty' words This is an important group of words which have very little meaning in their own right, because their meaning changes depending on the situation in which they're used. For instance, a word such as *him* is, in a sense, empty of meaning; you know it refers to some male individual, but you have no idea which. However, as soon as you see who I'm pointing to, the word becomes clear. All the 'pronouns' are like this – *he*, *she*, *you*, *mine*, and so on. So are such words as *here* and *there*, *this* and *that*. These are very useful words – as anyone knows who has struggled in a foreign language – because you can 'say' a great deal with these words and a few gestures. They can drive a parent to

distraction, though, as this conversation with a 2-year-old illustrates:

(*Sound of crash in another room.*)
Mother: Jamie, what's happened?
Jamie: It fall down.
Mother: What fell down, Jamie?
Jamie: That thing, there.
Mother: What thing?
Jamie: That one.

. . . and so on, often for some time, until mother is forced to go and see for herself.

During the second year, children learn words from all these fields, but some fields are more 'used' than others. In fact, around three-quarters of the words a child knows and uses belong to just two broad categories – the 'action' words and general 'naming' words (words for toys, clothes, objects, and so on). Also, some kinds of word are more likely to be understood rather than used. For instance, verbs such as *show*, *say* and *listen* are commonly used by parents, but less likely to be used by the children; whereas *bye-bye* and *night-night* are used by everyone. And parents use the location words (asking questions beginning with *where*, for instance) far more than the children do.

Still, it's an impressive performance, both in comprehension and production. If you keep a diary of a child's vocabulary learning, in its second year, you'll need quite a lot of paper.

What do they mean?

Mark jumps up with excitement as he hears a knock on the back door. His mother goes to open it, and there's the milkman. 'Dada', says Mark, in delight.

Mark may of course be right. Perhaps his father is a milkman. But there aren't enough milkmen to go round, so there has to be some other reason for this curious use of the word *dada*.

In fact, this 'extending' of a word to mean more than it should is a perfectly normal feature of language development during the second year, and it lasts until about halfway through the third year. To understand why children over-extend words in this way, you have to remember that there are two sides to learning a word. It's one thing to learn the 'shape' of the word – how it sounds. It's quite another to learn what the word means – that is, which objects and events in the real world it refers to. Children don't pick up a word with all its grown-up meanings neatly packaged inside it. They have to work out for themselves what it must mean. We have to do the same if we meet a new word in a foreign language, and there's no dictionary to help us out. Quite often, we get it wrong.

Children don't know any better either. Put yourself in their shoes. You hear a word being used to refer to an object. You look at the object, and you notice some feature of it – perhaps its size, colour, taste, sound, the way it moves, or (especially) its shape. So, naturally, you think the word refers to the feature you've spotted. A little later, along comes another object with the same feature. You therefore use the same word for that object too.

Let's apply this to the *dada* case. Perhaps the child has worked out that *dada* is the word you use whenever you see someone in trousers, or with a deep voice. Then along comes someone else with these features, and so they are *dadas* too.

Sometimes, it's quite a problem for adults to work out what the feature is that the child has focused on. Some children call cats and dogs *dadas*. One child pointed at the biscuit tin and said *dada*, though his father was not in the house, and hadn't been seen by the child for some hours. Perhaps in these cases, *dada* was the child's word for 'want' or 'I'm excited'?

You'll easily notice when words are over-extended in meaning, because the child will use a word to apply to a situation which doesn't match what goes on in the adult language. One child used *moon* to apply to the moon, a round cake, round shapes in books, round postmarks on envelopes, the letter O, and even the marks you make when blowing on a cold windowpane. Other common examples are *car* applied to all vehicles, or *dog* and *cat* used to apply to all animals, or all animals with four legs, or all animals with fur. Again, you don't know in advance which features the child is focusing on. You have to work it out. In the animal case, for example, researchers might show the child pictures of different animals, and see which ones the child spontaneously labelled *dog*. In one study, only animals with large tails were called *dog* – including horses, but excluding pigs (and some dogs, in fact). In another, only animals with four legs were allowed the name.

There's another way in which children change the meanings of adult words, but this is much more difficult to spot. Joanne, for example, walked over to her sandals, picked them up and said *shoe*, and every time her mother put her shoes on she would say the word – whatever type of shoe it was. You'd think from this that she'd learned the correct meaning. But she *wouldn't* use the word *shoe* to talk about her mother's shoes, or indeed about anyone else's shoes. You could put all the family shoes in a row, and say to Joanne, 'Show me the shoes', and she would unerringly go for her own, and leave the others. You could even ask, 'Are there any more shoes there, Jo?', and she'd shake her head.

What's happening here? This is the opposite of over-extending a word's meaning. Joanne has 'narrowed', or 'under-extended' the meaning of the word *shoe*. It no longer means 'footwear'; it means 'Joanne's footwear'. And similarly, other children have often been found to under-extend words. *Dog*, for example, might mean *only* the family dog. *Dada* might mean only the child's father – no one else can be a dada. Under-extensions are much more difficult to spot, though, because the child's use of the words is quite correct, as far as it goes. If you suspect an under-extension, you have to check it out by asking a set of questions of other objects which you'd refer to by the same word: 'Can that be a dog?', 'Is that a shoe?'

Sometimes you get both over-extension and under-extension at once. As his brother went out of a room and shut the door behind him, Mark pointed and said *door*. This seemed to be a new word, so, when his brother came back a few moments later, Mark's mother asked him 'What's that, Mark?', pointing to the open door. She got no answer. They shut the door, and Mark immediately said *door*! A little while later, Mark was heard to say *door* when someone put something away in a cupboard, and when someone put a handkerchief in a pocket. It seemed that he was using the word *door* to mean 'gone out of sight'. For Mark, only a 'shut door' could legitimately be called a *door* (under-extension), but anything which was shut away could be a door too (over-extension). Very subtle.

These are the main ways in which children get adult meanings wrong. There are others. Quite often, there's a complete mismatch between the child's meaning and the adult's. A child pointed at a cow and said *princess*. What was she remembering? What association of ideas was this? No one could work it out. Children who do this a great deal are very confusing to talk to!

It may take quite a long time for children to work out exactly what meaning a word has. One reason for this is that they aren't learning words one at a time. Everything's happening at once. If there's a nice clear contrast between two things, there won't be much of a problem: *cat* and *dog* are likely to be sorted out early on because of the obvious differences between them. And, as the child acquires more vocabulary, more of these differences will emerge. But with many words it's much more difficult trying to work out what the crucial distinctions are – what's the difference between *go* and *come*, *big* and *tall*, *behind* and *beneath*, *green* and *blue*, or *cup* and *glass*? Also, children may have been able to work out the exact meaning of a word when they hear adults use it, but still carry on using the wrong word when they speak. One child, for instance, picked out the right picture of *apple* every time, and never mixed it up. But he still talked about several other round objects as apples (tomatoes, balls, and so on). It took quite a while before his production 'caught up' with his comprehension.

Of course, parents help in all of this. They help by pointing out contrasts to the child. They say things like, 'That's not a cat, that's a dog', and then they explain: 'Listen, it goes woof. Pussy-cats go miaow.' Parents are very good at 'going on' about something in a relevant way. If their child says 'There green car', they go on to talk about cars of other colours, drawing the child's attention to the contrast. They are also good at instinctively choosing the word which will be most useful to the child. A dog could be labelled in many different ways (*Rover*, *animal*, *dog*, *terrier*, *long-haired terrier*), and parents tend to find the word which is at the right level, in a particular situation – not too general, not too specific. If an 18-month-old asks 'What that?', pointing to a dog, most parents would reply 'It's a dog', rather than 'It's an animal' (too general) or 'It's a long-haired terrier' (too specific). They wouldn't give that reply if an adult asked. 'What is it?' asks auntie, pointing to a newly purchased dog. 'It's a dog' is not the right answer – not unless you don't like auntie!

Grammar on the move

From around 12 months, when first words come, there is a period when children's utterances are no longer than a single word. One child throws a toy car on the floor and says *Gone*. Another stretches out a hand and says *More*. A third points at a toy and says *Teddy*. Sometimes they produce longer-sounding utterances – such as *allgone* or *ready-steady-go* – but these are deceptive. They have been learned as whole phrases. The child uses them as if they were single words, even though adults know differently.

This 'one-word stage' usually lasts around 6 months, though some children stay in it for longer. It's a stage when they start building up a vocabulary, as we've seen. But they also begin to use their new words in a variety of different ways, laying the foundations for their future grammatical abilities. Apart from this, there's very little that can be said about the 'grammar' of one-word utterances at this point. We can't analyse these words into parts (as we can with later words, such as *un-happy* or *walk-ing*). There are no endings on words yet. And it's not always easy to tell what part of speech a word is, because the meaning is often unclear. Still, some estimates have been made. About 60 per cent of one-word utterances seem to have a naming function ('nouns'), and about 20 per cent express actions. But under the heading of 'actions', we have to include more than just verbs. When a child says *In!*, gesturing violently, telling his mother where to put something, we have to interpret this as an 'action' utterance, even though the part of speech is a preposition.

One thing you *can* say about the one-word stage: these utterances are very similar to sentences, even though they've only got one word. Some people actually think of them as one-word sentences – 'holophrases', they call them. *Gone* would be thought of as equivalent to 'It's gone', *More* as 'I want more', and so on. Of course, the child isn't 'leaving out' the other words in these sentences – he hasn't learned enough language to do that yet – but he is certainly using these words *as if* they were sentences.

Sometimes there's quite clear evidence of a child's ability to do this. Fifteen-month-old Steven was in his play-pen towards the end of the day, when it was time for his father to come home. He heard the noise of a car outside and he listened carefully. *Dada?*, he said, with a rising melody, as if he were asking the question 'Is that daddy?'. A few seconds later, his father came into the room and Steven pointed, saying triumphantly, *Dada!* Here the descending melody on the word made it quite clear that he meant 'There's daddy'. And then, as you might expect, the tone of voice became higher and more insistent, as he lifted up his arms and said *Da-da!* – undoubtedly meaning 'Pick me up, daddy'. Here, then, we have the same word being used in three different functions. At a later stage in development, we would call these three functions 'Question', 'Statement' and 'Command'. At this stage, the sentences don't have the grammatical shape an adult could give them, but they have the force of real sentences nonetheless.

When, then, does *real* grammar start? Most people say: when

Ady horsie	hat off	my hat
baby bed	hat on	my teddy
baby cry	her coat	my tractor
baby doll	here is	she cold
baby drink	horsie mummy	she hair
baby hat	in there	shut door
baby here	is here	silly hat
baby lie	it gone	that bath
baby like	it off	that car
baby mummy	kiss doll	that hat
Bluey here-y'are	look elephant	that horsie
Bluey where	milk gone	there Bluey
comb hair	more toy	there teddy
come out	mumma back	toy gone
daddy there	mumma drink	waking up
dolly there	mummy off	want on
drink dolly	mummy there	where Bluey
gone milk	mummy toy	where inside
got it	my apple	where there
hat mummy	my bed	you bed

the child starts to string two words together. At around 18 months. It's a stage which moves very quickly, once it starts. To show this, all you have to do is listen carefully to the enormous range of two-word sentences used by a child who's been in this stage for only a few weeks. Christine Howe did this as part of a research study. On p. 76 are all the different two-word sentences used by one of her children, Victoria, at age 1;9 *in one hour*!

The sentences weren't spoken in this order, of course; Howe has put them into alphabetical order for convenience. Now that she has, several interesting features of this 'two-word' style stand out. For instance, various sets of sentences 'go together', because they all begin with the same word – *baby* and *mummy*, especially. Several other sentences all end with *there*, though this pattern is obscured by the alphabetical order. It's almost as if the child picks up a certain pattern and 'rings the changes' on it. You can sometimes hear children of this age going through a litany of sentences all beginning or ending with the same word, almost as if they were drilling themselves.

Another point to note is that the order of the words usually corresponds to what you'd expect in an adult sentence: the child says *my bed* and *got it*, and not *bed my* and *it got*. Sometimes you get both orders: for instance, she says both *hat mummy* and *mummy toy*. And sometimes the order isn't quite what you'd expect – such as *gone milk* and *Bluey where*. But on the whole, Victoria seems to have learned a lot about the main patterns of English word order – and she's only 1;9.

Children produce many two-word sentences, but what are they trying to say when they use them? Several child language investigators have made detailed studies of the meanings conveyed by such sentences. Here are some of these meanings, illustrated from Victoria's speech.

an Actor performs an Action	*baby cry, mumma drink*
an Action affects an Object	*comb hair, shut door*
an Object is given a Location	*baby here, there teddy*
an Object is given a Possessor	*my apple, mummy toy* (= 'mummy's toy')
an Object is made Specific	*that car*
an Object or Person is Described	*she cold, silly hat*

Many of Victoria's sentences can be explained with reference to these meanings. On the other hand, at this stage you'll always find several sentences where it isn't easy to say what a child is getting at. For instance, what does *look elephant* mean? Is Victoria telling us to look at the elephant? Or is she telling the elephant to look at us? Or is she saying that the elephant is looking at something? Or is she saying, 'Look! There's an elephant!'? Again, what does *hat mummy* mean? Does it mean 'mummy has a hat', or 'I see a hat and I see mummy', or 'there's a hat on mummy's head'? Usually, when you hear these sentences in real life, the situation makes it obvious which meaning the child intends. Sentences such as *it off* and *want on* will be clear enough when you see what the child is doing. But sometimes, even the visual clues don't sort out the ambiguity. You mustn't expect to understand *everything* that the child says in this stage, as this parent discovered:

Child: Daddy car.
Mother: What's that darling? Daddy's in his car?
Child: No. Daddy car.
Mother: What do you mean. You've just seen daddy's car?
Child: (*insistent*): No. Daddy car!
Mother: I don't know what you mean, darling. Daddy's at
   work. His car isn't here.
(*Child takes mother into the other room, where he points to a
   chair lying on its side.*)
Child: Look. Daddy car.
(*Mother finally realizes he's playing at being in daddy's car.*)

Life is full of such conversations at the two-word stage.

Now that sentences are becoming longer, it is possible to begin to make some simple analyses of what children say, from a grammatical point of view. Real grammar comes in English when children start to change the order of words to express different meanings, when *tickle man* means one thing, and *man tickle* means another. When children reach this stage in their development, we can start talking about their language using precise terms, such as 'subject', 'verb', and 'object'. *Tickle man* is 'verb + object'. *Man tickle* is 'subject + verb'. Similarly, this stage sees the emergence of some of the language's word endings – especially the *-ing* ending

on verbs, and the -s plural ending on nouns. Victoria had neither
of these at 1;9. But I once studied a child who at 1;8 was already
saying *man running*, *brush sweeping*, *see cats*, and *my shoes*.

The same principle applies to word endings. We can say that
children have learned a word ending only when they show in
their speech that they know what the difference is between using
it and not using it. You can test this out for yourself by getting a
child to name objects as you show them. Make sure that they've
got the hang of the game first. Then show them one shoe and see
what they say. It ought to be *shoe*. Next, do something else, to
take their mind off shoes. After a while, show them two shoes,
and see what they say. If they've learned the difference between
singular and plural, they ought to say *shoes*. If they haven't,
they'll still say *shoe*.

However, you might have an objection to this procedure. You
might be thinking: how do we know that the child hasn't simply
learned *shoe* off by heart for one shoe, and *shoes* off by heart for
more than one shoe? If that were so, they wouldn't really know
the difference between singular and plural at all. This is a good
point. But you can get round this problem by carrying out the
same experiment, using words you've made up instead of real
words. This is what Jean Berko did in a famous early experiment
on child language, though she was working with much older
children. She presented the children with a strange-looking animal
which she called a *wug*. Then she showed a picture of two of the
animals and prompted the child to say what was in the picture:
'There are two – ?' If the children had learned the plural ending,
they would say *wugs*. This couldn't be the result of learning off by
heart, of course, because the children would never have heard
the word before.

Children at the two-word stage are rapidly getting to grips with
grammar. They've learned a great deal about where words go in
sentences, and how they 'go together'. They're using some quite
subtle features, such as prepositions (*in there*, *on head*), possession
words (*my cat*), and pronouns (*she cold*, *her gone*, *it there*, *me
sore*). The sentences aren't very complex yet, of course, but the
scaffolding of grammar is there, waiting to be used for more
ambitious sentence building.

Two other points about this stage of grammatical development.

If you decide to look out for two-word sentences, beware! Not every sequence of two words is a two-word sentence. If I say quickly *John! Elephants!*, I am running together two *one-word* sentences. The same point applies to children at the beginning of this stage. They often lead up to a two-word sentence gradually – first stringing together a series of one-word sentences, each with its own melody and separated by a pause. At 1;5, one child said, in quick succession: *Daddy. Daddy. Car. Daddy. Gone. Car. Daddy.* There were no two-word sentences here. A few days later, she was saying such sentences as *Daddy gone* and *Gone car*, without pauses between the words, and giving each its own melody and rhythm. Now she had moved on to the two-word stage. But no one had noticed the point at which her sequence of two one-word sentences had changed into one two-word sentence.

How do they sound?

This chapter has listed many words and expressions used by children in their second year, but it's done so in normal spelling, which of course gives the wrong impression about their pronunciation. Words sound anything but normal, in the early months of the second year and, although great progress is made throughout this year, pronunciations still sound extremely immature at the end of it.

To begin with, children don't have the ability to make many sounds. Some have just two or three consonants and a single vowel. For instance, John at 13 months was able to use [b], [d] and [a] and nothing else. He was able to say only [ba], [da] and [a] – he couldn't manage the consonants after the vowel. But, armed with these three pronunciations, he was still able to express over a dozen words. For instance, *dog*, *car* and *there* all came out as [da]; and *daddy* and *dinner* came out as [dada]. You had to keep a careful eye on the situation, to see what he was talking about. If [da] came floating in from the other room, you wouldn't know whether he'd seen a car or a dog.

Gradually, as children learn to use more sounds, they become able to make more distinctions between words. John at 14 months had added [m], [g] and [u] to his repertoire, and that increased his stock of words enormously. He could then say such words as

[ma], [mu], [ga], [gu], [da] and [du], as well as [dada] and [mama], and he even managed to put some consonants at the end – [dud] and [dad]. It became much easier to follow him as a result. A few months later, he had learned over a dozen consonants and vowels and was distinguishing several hundred words.

It's not possible to predict *exactly* which sounds are going to be learned first by a child, and which next. Children can be very different. Some have favourite sounds which they try to introduce into almost every word. Others don't like certain sounds, and keep away from them. Some like to repeat sounds (see p. 86); others don't. Some drop the sounds at the end of words; others take great care to put them in. Faced with all these differences, it's very difficult to draw up a general order for the learning of sounds in a language.

Nonetheless, several people have tried, and they've found a number of interesting trends, which apply to many words produced by many children. For instance, consonant sounds made at the lips are likely to appear very early on in development. And 'stopped' consonants (such as [b] and [d]) also appear very early on. It's been noticed, too, that in most cases children are more likely to use consonants correctly at the *beginnings* of words. Consonants at the ends of words emerge much later (though there's an exception here in the case of the friction sounds, such as [f] or [s], which tend to appear at the end of words first). In 1971, David Olmsted published a survey of 100 children: this showed that, during the second year, [p], [b], [k], [n], [f], [d], [g], [m] and [h] were commonly used at the beginnings of words, but only the first five of these were common at the end. He also found that at least eight vowels were usually in use by the end of the year: [i] (as in *sit*), [ii] (as in *seat*), [a] (as in *cat*), [u] (as in *put*), [o] (as in *hot*), [oo] (as in *more*), [aa] (as in *car*) and [ai] (as in *my*).

Surveys of emerging sounds in young children have to be huge, if any reliable conclusions are to be drawn, because of the large amount of variation between individual children. On the other hand, despite these variations, it's not too difficult to draw conclusions about the *way* in which children change the sounds of the language, when they attempt to use them. Here are some of the most common changes they introduce.

– They don't like friction sounds, such as [f], and prefer to replace them by stopped sounds. That's why many children say [tii] for *sea*, or [pi] for *fish*.

– They don't like to produce sounds towards the back of the mouth, preferring to replace these by sounds made at the front of the mouth. This results in such pronunciations as [don] for *gone*, or [tii] for *key*.

– They prefer to use [w] and [j] sounds in place of the more difficult [l] and [r] sounds, as when *leg* is pronounced [jeg].

– As words become longer, they show a strong tendency for sounds in one part of a word to alter the pronunciation of sounds in other parts of the word. The sounds 'harmonize', as when the [d] in *dog* falls under the influence of the [g], so that the whole thing is pronounced [gog].

– They don't like 'clusters' of consonants, such as [tr] or [spr], replacing these by single consonants. So, *sky* often becomes [kai], and *tree* becomes [tii].

– They don't like consonants at the ends of words, preferring to leave them out. Thus, *hat* is commonly pronounced [ha], *bus* becomes [bu], and so on.

– They don't like quiet syllables in a word, preferring to drop them, as when *banana* becomes [nana], or *giraffe* becomes [raf].

– They *do* like to repeat syllables, so that *ball* can become [bobo], and *moo* becomes [mumu] (see p. 86).

One other point should be borne in mind when you begin to listen carefully to the pronunciation of a young child. Don't expect the pronunciation to be the same every time the child says it. In fact, children frequently vary the way they say things at this age. One day *dog* comes out as [da]; the next day (or even the next utterance) it comes out as [di], [dod], or some other form. Parents are sometimes surprised at this, but they shouldn't be. After all, everyone is a bit shaky, when they learn their first words in a new language. Still, it *is* remarkable just how variable some children are. One child of 1;5 had no less than six different versions of the word *window*. He would switch from one to the other quite at random, until several weeks later he settled down to use one of them.

Why do children vary the pronunciation of their words so much? Presumably because they are trying to work out how to relate the few sounds they can use to the 'target' sounds in the adult words. If you have six sounds at your disposal, and only six, and you want to say an adult word which contains sounds you can't do, all you can do is try out different combinations of the six you've got until you find something that works. In due course, people will begin to understand you, as your versions become more recognizable, but it may take a while.

There are lots of immaturities in the pronunciation of children in the second year, but there are always reasons for the errors they make. You'll begin to get a sense of this, if you start writing down the sounds they *do* use, alongside the sounds they *should* use. There are always some neat correspondences. You'll always find a pattern in the way a child plots a course through the maze of English pronunciation. But remember, if you decide to do some listening for sounds, you won't succeed without two things: a tape recorder (see p. 20) and a quiet time of day to listen in. And a sharp ear as well.

To conclude

As the second birthday approaches, most children have built up a core vocabulary of a couple of hundred words. They've learned to join these words together into simple sentences. And they can cope with an increasing number of sounds – at least a dozen, and perhaps as many as 20. But despite this great progress, 2-year-old language is still noticeably immature. It's probably the cutest period of language development, as these tots charm us all with their struggles to make longer sentences, bigger words and more complex sounds. But it doesn't last long. The third year is on the horizon, and that's serious.

Feature 4 | What is *gone*?

Gone (or *allgone*) is one of the commonest words used by children during their second year. When do they say it, and what does it mean? The obvious answer is that the word means 'something has disappeared', just as it does in the adult language. But the obvious answers are rarely the correct ones in language acquisition.

In a 1984 study by Alison Gopnik, nine children from the Oxford area were recorded during their second year. Three of them were audiotaped at home for an hour every fortnight; the remaining six were videotaped at home for half an hour every month over a 6-month period. Each of the children used *gone* spontaneously at some time or other, and altogether Gopnik collected 378 instances.

Almost all of the utterances (94 per cent, in fact) took place in one of four situations. The first situation was the obvious one: the children said *gone* when they saw an object, and the object then disappeared. But only 40 per cent of the cases were of this kind. Moreover, there were many ways in which an object could disappear from view. In some cases, the object itself moved, as when a ball rolled out of sight or a block was posted inside a letter-box. Sometimes, a screen came in front of the object, as in peek-a-boo games. Sometimes the object stayed still and the *children* moved, turning away from the object so that they couldn't see it. Or they said *gone* while picking up the object and placing it to one side. In all cases, the children were plainly expecting the object to reappear. Hiding-and-finding games are really popular at this age. And objects which move out of sight and don't reappear as expected (such as a ball, or a reluctant cat) can be a source of fury.

In 30 per cent of cases the children said *gone* when they searched for a missing object. Rachel said it when looking for her doll; Harriet when searching for the correct hole in a posting box. In such cases, the child doesn't need to have seen the object go.

You can hide an object without the child's knowledge, and when the disappearance is noticed, *gone* will often be said. Surprisingly they will even say *gone* about objects they have never actually seen, but whose existence they have deduced. One child took a set of beakers, and placed one inside another, until they were all used up. There was still a space in the smallest beaker, so she looked for another to put in it. *Gone*, she said, about this missing beaker, though none had ever existed. Another child searched for a pocket in his mother's apron. There was no pocket. *Gone*, he said.

In 20 per cent of cases, *gone* was used to comment on an empty container – after pouring all the pegs out of a tin, for example. This is an unsurprising use of the word, for it is similar to the situations in which an object is placed out of sight. What might seem more surprising is that the children often said the word when they looked inside a container which was *already empty*. For instance, Harriet looked in an empty doll's crib and said *gone*. Jonathan looked in the empty cab of a toy tractor and said *gone*. They expected an object to be there, and expressed their surprise when they found it wasn't.

In just 4 per cent of cases (15 occasions), the children used *gone* when objects were suddenly transformed. This happened most dramatically when something fell down, such as a carefully constructed tower of bricks. Henry said *gone* when his mother folded up her ironing board; Jonathan, when the cars of a toy train came apart. This use of the word was heard only at early ages.

How can these uses of *gone* be summarized? To the young child, the word means more than just 'disappeared'. It means something like 'I don't perceive something any more, and it should be there'. The object may be perfectly visible to everyone else in the room, but the child disregards that possibility. It's really quite a sophisticated, abstract notion which children express with this word – a mixture of what they perceive and what they believe. It's their word. There's nothing in the adult language quite like it.

Feature 5 | Let's reduplicate

During the second year, children always spend a certain amount of their time reduplicating. But don't panic: there are no clones involved. I'm not talking about the number of children in the family, only about the nature of the sounds within a word.

Reduplication takes place when children pronounce the different syllables of a word in the same way. Usually, at this age, these words have two syllables. *Water*, for example, might come out as [wowo]. *Bottle* might be [bubu]. Sometimes, the words sound quite unlike their adult counterparts. One child pronounced *window* as [mumu], for instance.

Of course, some of the words would have had identical syllables anyway – such as *bye-bye* and *night-night*. But most don't. And often children are so keen on reduplicating that they take words with just *one* syllable, and reduplicate that nonetheless. *Ball*, for example, emerges as [bobo].

Not all children reduplicate to the same extent. Some do it on nearly every word. Others do it on just a few words. Some do it mainly on words containing several syllables. Others do it on single-syllable words also. Some do it for a few days. With others, it lasts for months.

You can see the difference between children if I draw up two lists taken from a child who reduplicated a lot, and a child who did very little. They're based on a study carried out by Richard Schwartz and others published in 1979 (see p. 87). The first child has 10 complete reduplications, and 5 more words where there is just a small change between the first and second syllable. The other child has just one reduplicated word.

Why do they do it? Are they playing with sounds – and getting some practice in – as they did at the babbling stage (p. 45)? Possibly; but there's more to it than this. Reduplicated words may be a real help to children, as they try to cope with the pronunciation of more complicated words. It must be a lot easier to remember and pronounce [mimi] than [windou], for instance. It may also help

Child 1		Child 2	
Christmas	didi	*Snoopy*	supi, nupi
necklace	neke	*necklace*	nekis
hungry	hun	*hungry*	hanki
chip	ti	*chip*	tip
water	wowo	*water*	wot
chicken	kika	*chicken*	chik
banana	mimi	*drop*	dap
thank you	dete	*sock*	sap
sister	sisa	*Francie*	fati
belly button	beba	*hospital*	pit
mouth	mamav	*hair*	heir
clock	kak	*truck*	tak
candy	kei	*kitten*	kiki
money	mimi	*powder*	pav
house	didi	*pencil*	peta
Tigger	tidi	*burger*	bega
scissors	didi	*outside*	ausaid
take	keke	*boat*	bot
Angie	nano	*Eleanor*	ano

them to pronounce some of the syllables and sounds they find difficult, especially the sounds which occur at the ends of words. If you're trying to say *duck*, and you say [dukduk], you have two chances to get that final [k] sound right.

Reduplication could also help in another way. It might be a way of giving children the chance to master the pronunciation of words in stages. If we could see into the workings of the child's brain we might find some subconscious reasoning like this: '*Water*. Hmm. That's a two-syllable word with a lot of complicated sounds inside. I'll never manage it. But if I can get the syllables out, at least, then that's a start. That gives me a foothold. I can work on the individual sounds later. Here goes: [wowo]. That wasn't too bad. People seemed to understand me, anyway. Now, let's have another look at that middle sound, which didn't seem quite right . . .' If reality is at all like this, you can see the value of reduplication. It would be a way of speeding up the whole process of pronunciation learning at this stage.

Of course, it won't go on for ever. If you reduplicate all the time, there's a severe limit to what you can say! If *ball* is [bobo], and *baby* is [bobo], and *spoon* is [bobo], and so on, life is going to get very boboring – and confusing, after a while. So pressure is bound to build up on the child to stop reduplicating sooner or later, and to start distinguishing pronunciations more precisely. Few children keep it up after the age of 2.

Feature 6 | 'Fis' and 'tum'

Otherwise known as *fish* and *come*. They illustrate an important effect which can be noticed during the second year, and which can last for quite some time. Here's a story from a study by Neil Smith. The child is 4.

Father: What does [maus] mean?
Child: Like a cat.
Father: Yes: what else?
Child: Nothing else.
Father: It's part of you.
Child: (*disbelief*)
Father: It's part of your head.
Child: (*fascinated*)
Father (*touching child's mouth*): What's this?
Child: [maus].

What this story draws attention to is the difference between what children hear and what they can say. The child's pronunciation of the word *mouth* is [maus] – but he won't accept an adult pronouncing the word in this way. His father has got to say *mouth* with a *th* sound at the end, if he wants the child to understand.

There are other cases on record where children have gone further, and actually rejected their own pronunciation. The first study to point this out was carried out by Jean Berko and Roger Brown in 1960. They talked to a child who called his inflated plastic fish a *fis*. They imitated this pronunciation, and said to him: 'This is your *fis*?' 'No,' said the child, 'my *fis*.' They did this several times, and each time the child rejected his own pronunciation, when it was said by the adult. In the end, the adult gave in. 'That is your *fish*?' 'Yes,' said the child, 'my *fis*.'

Eve Clark reports another story of this kind. A child wanted to go on a trip to a 'mewwy-go-wound'. He was teased by an older

child, who said: 'David wants to go on the mewwy-go-wound.'
No,' said David firmly, 'you don't say it wight'!

These are all examples of children knowing far more about the pronunciation of a word than their own pronunciation gives them credit for. You can see this ability, too, in the way that children are able to distinguish adult words that they themselves pronounce in the same way. One child pronounced *jug* and *duck* identically, as [gak], but she never had any trouble telling the two words apart. 'Which one's a *jug?*' she was asked, showing her several pictures of objects – and she would point to the jug. 'Which one's a *duck?*' – and again she would have no trouble.

Young children, it seems, don't much like their own immature way of pronouncing things. With older children, you can actually show this by tape recording what they say, then playing it back to them to see whether they can understand it. Barbara Dodd did this with three-year-olds. She found that they failed to understand over half of their own mispronounced words. By contrast, when she played a tape of an adult saying the same words, they hardly ever got them wrong.

It rather looks as if the 'shape' of a word that children store in their brain is more like the adult version than the child's one, otherwise they wouldn't be able to make distinctions of this kind. But this doesn't mean that you can persuade children to pronounce their words more correctly than they do. Just because they can *hear* a difference doesn't mean to say they'll be able to *make* it, and there's no point in trying to force them.

Force them? It happens. Samuel Butler tells such a story, in Chapter 22 of *The Way of All Flesh* (1903). It's a sad tale, which shows how easy it is to break all the rules of good language fostering.

In the course of the evening they came into the drawing-room, and, as an especial treat, were to sing some of their hymns to me, instead of saying them, so that I might hear how nicely they sang. Ernest was to choose the first hymn, and he chose one about some people who were to come to the sunset tree. I am no botanist, and do not know what kind of tree a sunset tree is, but the words began, 'Come, come, come; come to the sunset tree for the day is past and gone.' The tune was rather pretty and had taken Ernest's fancy, for he was unusually fond of music and had a sweet little child's voice which he liked using.

He was, however, very late in being able to sound a hard 'c' or 'k', and, instead of saying 'Come,' he said 'Tum, tum, tum.'

'Ernest,' said Theobald, from the arm-chair in front of the fire, where he was sitting with his hands folded before him, 'don't you think it would be very nice if you were to say "come" like other people, instead of "tum"?'

'I do say tum,' replied Ernest, meaning that he had said 'come'.

Theobald was always in a bad temper on Sunday evening. Whether it is that they are as much bored with the day as their neighbours, or whether they are tired, or whatever the cause may be, clergymen are seldom at their best on Sunday evening; I had already seen signs that evening that my host was cross, and was a little nervous at hearing Ernest say so promptly 'I do say tum', when his papa had said he did not say it as he should.

Theobald noticed the fact that he was being contradicted in a moment. He got up from his arm-chair and went to the piano.

'No, Ernest, you don't,' he said, 'you say nothing of the kind, you say "tum", not "come". Now say "come" after me, as I do.'

'Tum,' said Ernest, at once; 'is that better?' I have no doubt he thought it was, but it was not.

'Now, Ernest, you are not taking pains: you are not trying as you ought to do. It is high time you learned to say "come", why, Joey can say "come", can't you, Joey?'

'Yeth, I can,' replied Joey, and he said something which was not far off 'come'.

'There, Ernest, do you hear that? There's no difficulty about it, nor shadow of difficulty. Now, take your own time, think about it, and say "come" after me.'

The boy remained silent a few seconds and then said 'tum' again.

I laughed, but Theobald turned to me impatiently and said, 'Please do not laugh, Overton; it will make the boy think it does not matter, and it matters a great deal', then turning to Ernest he said, 'Now, Ernest, I will give you one more chance, and if you don't say "come", I shall know that you are self-willed and naughty.'

He looked very angry, and a shade came over Ernest's face, like that which comes upon the face of a puppy when it is being scolded without understanding why. The child saw well what was coming now, was frightened, and, of course, said 'tum' once more.

'Very well, Ernest,' said his father, catching him angrily by the shoulder. 'I have done my best to save you, but if you will have it so, you will,' and he lugged the little wretch, crying by anticipation, out of the room. A few minutes more and we could hear screams coming from the dining-room, across the hall which separated the drawing-room from the dining-room, and knew that poor Ernest was being beaten.

'I have sent him up to bed,' said Theobald, as he returned to the drawing-room, 'and now, Christina, I think we will have the servants in to prayers', and he rang the bell for them, red-handed as he was.

Feature 7 | The first fifty words

By around 18 months, most children come to use a spoken vocabulary of about 50 words. Some of the words will be used just once; others will be used several times. Which words will they be? Is there any possible way of predicting them?

The answer seems to be no – at least, not as far as specific words are concerned. (It is easier to predict the 'types' of words they will use: see p. 68.) There is an enormous amount of individual variation between children, and even some of the most 'obvious' candidates (such as *mummy* and *daddy*) aren't always present in a child's earliest lexicon. The variation is immediately apparent if we look at the first 50 words of different children.

Three American children, Daniel, Will and Sarah, were studied in the early 1980s by Carol Stoel-Gammon and Judith Cooper as part of a project on the development of pronunciation. All three were the first-born children of middle-class parents. The data were collected in the children's homes by their mothers, who took notes of their child's vocalizations every other day. Fortnightly tape recordings were also made.

Each child used a first word at a different age and took a different period of time to reach 50 adult-like words. Sarah's first word was at 11 months; and both Daniel and Will began at 12 months and 2 weeks. Daniel took 4 months to reach 50 words; Sarah took $5\frac{1}{2}$ months; and Will took $6\frac{1}{2}$ months.

There are few similarities in the vocabulary used: in fact, only eight words are shared by the three lists (*baby, daddy, hi, shoe(s), bye-bye, ball, more, mommy*). On the other hand, some of the differences can be explained by the way Daniel and Will seemed to display preferences for certain types of word. Will evidently likes repeated words, such as *pop-pop* and *mimi*; he would repeat other words in the list too, such as *coat-coat* and *go-go-go*. He's obviously a 'reduplicator' (see p. 86). But, above all, he liked to do this for names of things that made sounds, such as *moo-moo* and *beep-beep*. He would far rather use the name of the sound an animal makes than its real name. Daniel shows a little of this, but his preference is clearly for words which contain a [k] or [g], either in the middle or at the end. Fourteen of his words are like this: *rock, sock, clock, yuk,* and so on.

In Appendix 1 (p. 223) there's a page on which you can record your own child's first 50 words. As you fill it in, remember three points:

1. Several words will be pronounced in exactly the same way. In Daniel's speech, for example, *quack, rock, clock, cock, frog, whack, yuk, walk, block,* and *milk* were all pronounced [gak]. These identical pronunciations for different words are called 'homophones' (they are present in adult language, too, as with *bear* 'animal' and *bear* 'carry'). If you write down the child's pronunciation, therefore, remember to gloss its meaning as well, e.g. gak = duck.

2. You can't tell the meaning of a young child's words just by listening to them. You have to look carefully at the situation in which a word is used. Jane may point to a toy teddy and say [taa]. She may also point to the cat and say [taa]. If you weren't looking at the time, you might think that she was still talking about the teddy, and miss the fact that this was a new word. (Of course, there's always the possibility that she thinks the cat *is* a teddy!)

3. Don't be confused by the fact that some words will resemble two-word sentences, such as *what's that* and *don't throw* in the lists on p. 95. They aren't separate words, in fact. They've been picked up by the child as single spoken units, and they're pronounced in that way, and not as two separate words. *What's that,* for example, sounded more like [bizda]. Another common one is *all gone,* which is usually pronounced something like [ada]. I recall one child who used a *five*-word utterance as one of his 'first words': it was *one two three four five,* which he used when he wanted his parents to play their finger-tickling game. He pronounced it [tuufeef].

	Daniel		Sarah		Will
1	light	1	baby	1	uh-oh
2	uh-oh	2	mommy	2	alldone
3	what's that	3	doggie	3	light
4	wow	4	juice	4	down
5	banana	5	bye-bye	5	shoes
6	kitty	6	daddy	6	baby
7	baby	7	milk	7	don't throw
8	moo	8	cracker	8	moo
9	quack (quack)	9	done	9	bite
10	cookie	10	ball	10	three
11	nice	11	shoe	11	hi
12	rock (NOUN)	12	teddy	12	cheese
13	clock	13	book	13	up
14	sock	14	kitty	14	quack-quack
15	woof-woof	15	hi	15	oink-oink
16	daddy	16	Alex	16	coat
17	bubble	17	no (no)	17	beep-beep
18	hi	18	door	18	keys
19	shoe	19	dolly	19	cycle
20	up	20	what's that	20	mama
21	bye-bye	21	cheese	21	daddy
22	bottle	22	oh wow	22	siren sound
23	no	23	oh	23	grrr
24	rocky (VERB)	24	button	24	more
25	eye	25	eye	25	off
26	nose	26	apple	26	tick tock
27	fire	27	nose	27	ball
28	hot	28	bird	28	go
29	yogurt	29	alldone	29	bump
30	pee-pee	30	orange	30	pop-pop (*fire*)
31	juice	31	bottle	31	out
32	ball	32	coat	32	heehaw
33	whack (whack)	33	hot	33	eat
34	frog	34	bib	34	neigh-neigh
35	hello	35	hat	35	meow
36	yuk	36	more	36	sit
37	apple	37	ear	37	woof-woof
38	Big Bird	38	night-night	38	bah-bah
39	walk	39	paper	39	hoo-hoo (*owl*)
40	Ernie	40	toast	40	bee
41	horse	41	O'Toole	41	tree
42	more	42	bath	42	mimi (*ferry*)
43	mommy	43	down	43	s: (*snake*)
44	bunny	44	duck	44	ooh-ooh (*monkey*)
45	my	45	leaf	45	yack-yack (*people talking*)
46	nut	46	cookie	46	hohoho (*Santa*)
47	orange	47	lake	47	bye-bye
48	block	48	car	48	doll
49	night-night	49	rock	49	kite
50	milk	50	box	50	Muriel

Feature 8 | Asking questions

When do children first start to ask questions? And which questions do they ask first? This was one of the main topics to be investigated by child language researchers in the 1960s, and it's continued to fascinate people since.

From the beginning of the second year, until well into the third, three main stages of development have been identified.

Stage 1 Children show signs of wanting to ask questions as early as the end of the first year. They haven't got any grammatical skills at that point, of course, but they are certainly able to convey a questioning meaning, by using the melody of the voice. This is something adults do as well. 'Lunch?' someone might ask. When this is written down you know it's a question because of the question mark. In speech, you know it's a question because the pitch of the voice is high and it rises as you say it. One child said *Dada?* upon hearing a noise outside at the time when daddy was expected home (see p. 76). Another held his drink over the edge of his high chair and said *Gone?* After he'd dropped it, he looked down at the mess he'd created, lowered his tone and said definitively, *Gone!*

Long sentences can be given a questioning intonation too. 'He's travelling to Athens by car?' someone might query. 'Yes, he's travelling to Athens by car.' Notice that it's the same sentence both times, as far as the grammar is concerned. The only thing which makes the first sentence a question and the second one a statement is the different tone of voice used. During the second year, children's sentences become longer too, and the same kind of questioning tone will be heard. *Daddy there?*, a child might say. Or *Teddy now?*

Stage 2 During the second year, children start to use question words; these are words such as *what, where, when* and *why. What* and *where* are usually the first two to emerge in a child's speech, often being used just on their own at around 15 or 18 months. Soon, they come to be used along with other words: *Where that?*, *Where car?*, *What that?*, *What doing?* They start asking *why*, *how*, and *who* questions some time afterwards. And *when* questions are later still.

Of course, asking questions is one thing. Understanding the questions adults ask *you* is quite another. Most children grasp first the meaning of questions which require a 'yes/no' answer (such as 'Can you see daddy?'), and questions beginning with *what* and *where*; but the order in which they learn the others isn't fully understood. For example, some learn the meaning of *why* questions before *who* questions. Others learn *who* before *why*. So, if you want to find out which question words a child understands, there's only one way to do it, and that's to ask a question, and see what happens. But be prepared for some strange replies, such as:

Parent: When did daddy go out?
Child: He's in the garden.

This child has taken the *when* question to be a *where* question, something that's very common in the early stages of question learning.

Stage 3 Questions become more complex, as the child moves into the third year. Sentences are longer now. *Where daddy going? What you doing in there?* This is the time when children discover the rule for turning English statements into questions. The rule is quite a simple one. To turn *That is a car* into a question, all you have to do is reverse ('invert') the order of the subject and verb: *Is that a car?* Children pick this rule up quite early in the third year for some questions, but it takes them longer in the case of others.

Questions which can be answered by 'yes' or 'no' seem to present no real problem. *Are you there?*, *Is Daddy in the garden?*, *Can I do that?*, and the like are quickly learned with the correct word order. But sentences beginning with a question word often seem to take longer to learn. Here, many children start by using such constructions as *Where daddy is going?* or *What you are doing?* Only later do they invert the order of subject and verb, to produce *Where is daddy going?* and *What are you doing?*

Why do these children make this error? Probably because a

sentence such as *Where is daddy going?* in fact contains *two* markers that it is a question. First there's the question word itself – *where*, in this case. Then there's the changed order of subject and verb – *is daddy*. Looking at it from the child's point of view, we can readily imagine a child 'thinking': 'If I've already said *where*, I've asked the question. I don't need to ask it all over again, by changing the word order!' It's a logical way of looking at things. Unfortunately, language doesn't work in a perfectly logical way. It often makes you do two things when only one would do. As children move into their third year, it must slowly dawn on them that, linguistically, it's a hard life.

Feature 9 | Colour words

When do children learn the names for colours? David Cruse studied his son, Pierre, and found several stages of development throughout the second year of life.

At age 1;3, Pierre had produced no colour words at all, nor was there any sign that these words were understood (though the parents often used them to the child). By contrast, Pierre was using several shape words: *round*, *square*, and even *triangle*!

His first colour word came at 1;4: *green*. Pierre seemed to use it as a real colour word, unlike those children who sometimes use their first colour words as if they were names of objects (for instance, pointing at the snow and saying *white*). But *green* wasn't used just to refer to things which were green. It referred to any bright thing, whatever its colour.

A month later, several colour words had been produced, usually as part of a two-word sentence. Pierre said *blue flower*, *green car*, *red tower*, *white spoon*, and *brown shoe*, for example. He now replied with colour words, when his parents asked him 'What colour is that?' However, the colour words seemed to be used randomly: there was little sign that he knew the exact meaning of any of the words. The flowers, for instance, were sometimes blue, sometimes not. Shoes were *brown shoes*, whether or not they were brown.

Pierre may not have known his colour *words*, at this stage, but he nonetheless knew the difference between colours. Many children are like this during their second year. How do we know he knew? There are several simple tests you can carry out, to see whether a child recognizes colours. For instance, take several blocks (or any toys) which are exactly the same apart from their colour. Choose one of them and show it to the child. Then, when the child isn't looking, put the block among the others. Children who have some memory for colours will be able to locate the block. But their ability to do this is often several months in advance of their ability to use colour words.

By 1;8, Pierre had begun to use some colour words

appropriately. He used *black* and *white* correctly when the situation showed a clear-cut contrast – such as a black cat next to a white cat. Many children in fact learn the *black/white* distinction first, presumably because the contrast of brightness is a very noticeable one. But when these words first appear, they are often used with reference to other colours as well. In Pierre's case, *black* was also used to refer to dark blue and dark brown; and *white* was used for yellow. This kind of over-extension is common in young children (see p. 72).

Other colour words were in use at this age but not very consistently. He correctly identified the colour of a few toys, items of clothing, and other familiar objects; but he still labelled less familiar objects at random. For example, a red toy car might be labelled correctly; but a red aeroplane in a picture would not. You will often find some inconsistency in the learning of colour words, and often it's not at all obvious why a child should be able to name the colour of one object correctly, and get the same label wrong on another. Some parents put it down to perversity. 'Ooh, you just don't want to play, do you?' said one mother, crossly, after her child had mislabelled some colours, after getting some right. But gradual learning seems in fact to be a quite normal thing.

At age 1;11, Pierre was able to use eleven colours, as follows:
green and *white* were being used correctly;
yellow was used more or less correctly;
red was used for red, and most of what adults would call 'orange';
blue was used for blue, but also most of purple and bluish grey;
black was used for black, and also for very dark brown;
pink was used for pink and pinkish grey;
orange was used only for yellowy-orange;
brown was used for all browns except the darkest shades, dull orange, and dull mauve;
grey was used only for the most neutral grey; anything tinted was labelled differently;
purple was used only for familiar objects of that colour.

Cruse's study stopped here, with the child at 1;11. Pierre has done very well in such a short time – better than many children, in fact. But there is still a great deal of learning to be done. The boundaries between several colours need to be made more precise: red and orange aren't clearly distinguished, and several of the darker shades are confused. *Purple* is being used in a very limited way. There is no sign of the more subtle colour distinctions. Also, there isn't perfect consistency. As with many 2-year-olds, Pierre is better at telling colours apart when he sees them side-by-side than when he sees a single colour. He is at the earliest stage of being able to differentiate hues, an ability which will continue to develop over several years.

We spend an awful lot of verbal time, in the second year, telling children what to do. David Bellinger, in a 1979 study, found that a *third* of the utterances mothers used to their children in the second year were attempts to direct their child's behaviour. After 2, the frequency with which they uttered these 'directive' utterances was much less. It doesn't take long to learn some obedience, it seems!

Bellinger also looked at the *way* in which mothers directed their children, between 1 and 5 years of age, to see whether there were any changes in their practice. There were. To show this, he classified their utterances into five types, ranging from the most direct to the most indirect.

1. The clearest type is a straightforward command: *Put those blocks away!*, *Come and sit down!*. Sometimes, the child's name is added, or a pronoun used: *Put that down, John!*, *You stop that!*.

2. A 'softened' version of a command uses the same grammar, but the melody of a question. We might write it: *Put those blocks away?* It's really a shorthand way of asking 'Will you put those blocks away?'.

3. Much less direct is the command which is phrased as a question. A parent might say, *Where do those blocks go?*, and is not expecting merely the answer *in the box*! This 'question' is in fact a veiled command, and woe betide the child who does not realize this and do something about it. Parents differ in their choice of question here. Some stress the child's ability: *Can you put those blocks away?*. Some stress the child's knowledge: *Do you know how to put blocks away?*. There are many variants.

4. Still less direct is the use of a statement, such as *Those blocks must be put away* or *Those dollies need to go on the shelf.* Such sentences don't actually ask or command anyone to do anything. But the implication is clear: whoever is in earshot had better do something about it.

5. The least direct command is one which doesn't necessarily

refer to the hoped-for action at all. A child might be tugging at a button attached to the side of a toy. *It's fixed on*, says the mother, which means, in effect, 'There's no point in carrying on pulling, so stop!'. This is quite a sophisticated kind of reply, which assumes that the child can work out the reasoning. It would cut no ice with a 2-year-old!

As this last comment suggests, it's likely that mothers will change the ways in which they tell their children to do things, as their children get older. And this is what Bellinger found. The first two types were very common at the beginning of the second year, but became much less frequent at later ages. The third type was particularly common in the second half of the second year. The fourth type became increasingly used after age 2. And the last type was frequent only at age 5. It seems that, as children get older, mothers rely more on sentences which 'suggest' rather than 'tell'.

It's interesting to see the way parental language changes, if one of these ways of telling doesn't work. Anthony, aged 4, picked up a pair of scissors from his mother's knitting bag. The mother started with a Type 5 directive: *Careful, Anthony, scissors are sharp.* That had no effect. She tried another Type 5: *You'll hurt yourself.* Anthony continued to study the scissors with great intensity. She shifted to a Type 4: *The scissors go in this bag, please.* Still no effect. Type 3: *Will you put those scissors down, please.* Said too gently, no effect. She skipped Type 2, and went directly to a fortissimo Type 1: *Anthony, put those scissors down this minute!* Effect.

Many parents keep a diary of their children's general development – when they crawled, sat up, walked, cut a tooth, and so on. These are Great Events, well worth writing down for posterity to admire. They may even be used in evidence, especially when there are other family members to be compared. Everyone finds them interesting to look back on; and they can be useful, too, if a child falls ill one day. Medical specialists will want to know about the early developmental history as part of their study of a condition, and it's very helpful to have a record to hand in a small notebook.

A diary of language development is no different – except that, if you keep it properly, you need a bigger notebook. Language isn't like other aspects of child development: there are far more points of detail to be learned, and everything happens in such a short time (see Chapter 1). People talk happily of 'milestones' of general development. With language, the metaphor isn't really appropriate: important developments take place, instead, every few yards. As a result, a systematically kept diary can quickly become voluminous. Few people keep such a diary going for long, unless they have a professional interest in doing so. One famous child language researcher, Werner Leopold, kept a diary on his daughter, Hildegard. When he finally published his analysis of the material, it took four large volumes.

You won't need a diary like that. Parent diaries of child language have to be extremely selective, if they're to be manageable. They're usually little more than a list of notable words, sentences, and anecdotes, written down when an opportunity arises. They often start as a child approaches the first words stage, and last a year or so. Few parents keep them going for much longer – either the novelty wears off or they run out of time (something which is very likely to happen when new brothers or sisters come on the scene). I've seen many dead diaries which begin well, but trail away into silence as a new birth approaches. On the other hand,

I've seen some beautifully kept diaries which have lasted until age 5 or 6 – one for every member of the family. Admittedly, in the case I'm thinking about, she was (as they say) an 'organized' mother. But it shows it can be done.

Even if you keep the diary going for just a few months, it's well worth doing. You'll get a great deal of pleasure out of the book a few years afterwards. So it's worth doing well. Keep the following points in mind.

1. This is a book which is going to have a lot of use, being continually picked up and put down. Moreover, it gets put down in odd places, such as in a bath, a bowl of porridge, or a dirty nappy. It therefore needs to be quite tough if it is to survive. Choose a notebook with hard covers, not one of the floppy ones.

2. Remember you need something to write with. There is nothing worse than hearing a verbal gem and being unable to write it down because you can't find an unbroken pencil, or a biro with ink in. By the time you've tracked one down, the gem can be forgotten or misremembered. It's no good keeping a pen in each room. They never stay in the right place, and they're no help when you go out. It's far easier to find a notebook with a pen(cil) attached, or to tie one to the spine of the book.

3. Once you've found a book, and a pen, and a baby, you can start the diary. Most people organize their diary chronologically: they begin at the baby's beginning, and every observation follows in sequence. If you work like this, get into the habit of putting the date before every entry – and age, too, for ease of reference later.

Some people like to organize their diary thematically: they have one section for vocabulary, another for grammar, another for sounds, and so on. Then, within each section, they write things down in chronological order. This is much more difficult to do successfully, and I really wouldn't advise it unless you've got some training in language analysis behind you, and are *very* organized.

4. The 'beginning' can be whenever you want. You can start early on in the first year if you wish, noting down the first signs of cooing and babbling, and the different kinds of sound which occur (see Chapter 2). Or you can note the developing way in which your child seems to understand you, before any words emerge at all. You say the name of a favourite toy, and the child looks in its direction. This is just as much a 'yardstone', worthy of record.

But first words provide the first big opportunity for diary keeping. When they start, you must expect to add new entries every couple of days. Remember to keep an eye on the situation in which the word is used. One day, the child may say *dog* while pointing to the dog; the next day, the same word might be used while pointing to the cat. You must make a note of the meanings as well.

5. Diary keeping isn't like tape recording (see p. 20). You can't do it at fixed intervals – standing over the child with notebook at the ready, like a journalist. The whole point is to jot things down as they come up, as accurately as you can.

Accuracy is a key issue. There's not much point in writing down what you *think* the child said, several hours later. A language diary is different from an ordinary diary, in this respect. People who keep a daily diary often write it up at the end of their day. They think back over the day, and summarize what went on. Language diaries can't be like this. They aren't impressions. They aren't summaries. They should be precise accounts of what the child said or understood – as precise as you can make them. And that means you must write things down at the earliest possible moment, preferably within seconds. It's so easy to forget what was said, even half a minute later. 'Did he say *catch a ball* or *catch the ball*? I can't remember.' It's very tempting to guess. 'Oh well, I expect it was *catch the ball*. It sounds more natural, anyway.' If you start doing this, you'll end up keeping a record of *your own* language, not the child's.

The biggest risk of all is that you read things into what the child says. *Kick ball* says the child – and you write down 'Kick a ball', 'kicking the ball', or the like. The child says *he running* – and you write down 'He's running'. It's only natural to read things in to a sentence, to imagine it as *you* would say it. You have to train yourself to listen as carefully as you can, and to be prepared for anything.

But don't be discouraged if you do listen carefully, and you still don't understand everything that the child says. According to some estimates, about a third of what children say in their second year isn't intelligible to anyone. And even older children (and adults) often say things so fast or incoherently that it's not possible to be sure exactly what was said. Even the experts have trouble at times. Child language researchers can spend hours listening over and over to a single piece of tape, to be sure that what they have written down is exactly what was said. You don't have to go so far, but beware of the problem.

6. Last, don't draw attention to yourself, as you write things down. Do it casually and out of sight, if possible. Children get self-conscious at a very early age, as anyone knows who has tried to get them to talk into a tape recorder. We don't want children to grow up thinking they're under permanent observation. The children's newspeak is interesting and fun, for all around – but don't turn your interest into a regime. Big Mother is Watching You? I hope not.

Mother: You run on ahead, and I'll catch up with you.
Jane (2;6): Whose head, mummy?

Mother (*going through the alphabet*): Say T.
Mary (3;6): T.
Mother: U.
Mary: U.
Mother: V.
Mary: V.
Mother: W.
Mary: Double me.

James (2;6) (*after furiously scratching his ear*): Oh look,
    mummy. My itch is gone now, and I got a wak out of it.

Mother: Don't argue!
Hugh (3;0): I don't argme.

Marcus (3;0) (*in train, approaching London*): Are we there
  yet?
Father: No, we're still in the outskirts.
(*Pause*)
Marcus: Have we reached the inskirts yet?

Michael (4;0) (*in bedroom*): Don't shut my door, mummy.
Mother: Well I have to close it, darling, because the light will
    keep you awake.
Michael: No, don't want you to.
Mother: I'll leave it ajar, then.
Michael: Can you leave it one and a half jars?

Father (*telling mother*): . . . so I took the wrong bus by
    mistake.
Francis (4;0) (*listening*): Yes, he took it by his-stake.

Mother (*hearing doorbell ring*): That'll be the greengrocer.
David (4;0): Is he green when he takes his coat off?

Mother: What's a vixen? Do you know?
Mary (6;0): A lady vicar.

Dena (8;0) (*on getting up in the morning*): I had a nightmare
. . . Well, it was a morningmare, really, 'cos it was five past
seven.

Commentary

These anecdotes have one thing in common. They show the child
grappling with one of the largest problems in language acquisition: how do you work out the meaning of a word from its
structure? In many of the cases, the children are applying their
previous linguistic knowledge, plus a touch of logic, to a new
word – and getting it wrong.

In three of the stories, they hear what they think is a pronoun
and, being knowledgeable about pronouns, they change it to the
appropriate person. This happens with *mistake, argue* and *W*. The
same sort of logic applies to *outskirts, nightmare* and *greengrocer,*
where they think the first part of the word can be used literally, as
it can in other circumstances.

In *ahead* and *ajar,* the children have thought they heard a well-
known combination – the indefinite article (*a*) + a familiar word,
as in *a head* and *a jar.* This is something which happens quite a lot
in English, whenever the (rather rare) *a-* prefix occurs. Adults
sometimes even make jokes on the same principle. We read on
the wall, *Be alert.* Underneath is written: *This country needs lerts.*

In the case of *wax,* James has analysed the word as a plural
because of the way *x* is pronounced as [ks]. *Sacks* gives you *sack,* so
wax gives you *wak.* This is quite common too. I recently heard,
There's another Mercede. But *vixen* is unexpected – as well as being a
delight! The only other words in the language which are like it are
ox/oxen and *child/children.* Perhaps Mary thought the *-en* part of
the word was an ending, therefore; but I can't think why she would
interpret it as female. Maybe she was having her mother on.

4 | The Third Year

The third year is truly remarkable from a linguistic point of view. So much progress is made. So many things happen at once. No other year can match it. That's the good news.

The bad news is that it's very difficult to keep track of everything when you're studying child language at this age. In a short book, it's impossible. So if you notice a linguistic feature emerging during this year which isn't discussed in this chapter, don't dismiss it. Limited space is the problem, is all.

You'll get an immediate sense of the linguistic leap children make if I list side by side some typical 2-year-old sentences and some typical 3-year-old sentences (taken from several children). It is a different world at 3.

Age 2	Age 3
Teddy on floor.	You put that on there.
That stuck now.	Me got lots of cars like Jimmy.
Mummy gone out.	Mummy want me to go in the garden.
No daddy go.	Where you going with that red shovel?
Open it.	Daddy comed to see me in the garden.
Put in box.	I can see mummy and daddy in the mirror.
Look my dollie.	Mary went in the Wendy house with me and Paul.
What doing it?	Why you do that for?
Fall down car.	Can me put it in like that?
My mouse eating.	It doesn't go that way, it goes this way.
More that in minute.	I got enough of those apples now.

The obvious difference is that the sentences at 3 are much longer. Three or four words per sentence are the average at age 2, with the occasional longer utterance. A year later, sentences of nine or ten words are not at all uncommon.

However, there's more to language development than merely increasing the length of a sentence. After all, it would be possible

"Well, if they *don't* go 'chuff-chuff' anymore, how *do* they go?"

KEVIN WOODCOCK

for a child's sentences to get longer simply by stringing together a series of nouns with the word *and*. *Me see a man and a car and a dog and a cat and a house* . . . Sentences could get infinitely long using this technique, but they wouldn't be saying very much. Far more important is the *reason* for the increase in length. Children's sentences get longer because they have more to say, and they need a wider range of construction with which to say them. The interesting thing about 3-year-old language is how varied it is. Many different kinds of structures are used, and the child combines words in creative and increasingly unpredictable ways.

Sentence parts

Probably the most important grammatical development is the way in which children gradually build up quite complicated sentences out of their component parts. Before 2, most sentences are limited to two main parts, as you can see from this dialogue, where this 21-month-old child wants to say a longer sentence but can't manage it. His mother has to say the whole sentence for him.

Child (*coming in from garden*): Daddy knee.
Mother: What's that, darling? What about daddy's knee?
Child: Fall-down daddy.
Mother: Did he? Where did he fall down?
Child: In-garden fall-down.
Mother: Daddy's fallen down in the garden! Poor daddy. Is he
   all right?
Child: Daddy-knee sore.
Mother: Daddy's fallen over and his knee's sore? I'd better
   come and see, hadn't I?

I've linked certain words with hyphens, in this example, to show how the sentences can be divided into two main parts, even though the child is using three or four words. The mother, though, doesn't find these two-part sentences enough. She wants more information. Her first question asks what happened to daddy's knee, and it produces a verb – *fall-down*. She then asks where this took place, and the result is a phrase expressing the location – *in-garden*. A third question establishes that all is not well with the knee. And so the conversation proceeds.

In conversations like this, the mother seems to be constructing the sentence her child is trying to say, using the clues provided by what the child actually says. Her questions and rephrasings are asking, in effect, 'Is this what you mean? Have I got it right? Can you tell me some more, so that I understand you correctly?' A mother's language, at this stage of development, is often like this – expanding what the child says into a bigger and better sentence. Some child language scholars think that it is very important to talk to a child in this way at this stage of development. They feel that these expansions are a means of showing the child fresh linguistic horizons. The parent accepts what the child says and then goes one better, producing a more advanced sentence which expresses the idea more clearly or acceptably. By doing this, parents show their children a more mature means of expression which, in due course, the children will learn to use.

If the mother were teaching English to foreigners, she would be doing very similar things. We might easily imagine a foreigner saying *Man fall-down*. The teacher might then correct the grammar and expand the sentence: 'The man's fallen down in the garden.' Of course, parents are not consciously 'teaching' their children at this age. But the similarities between what they do and what teachers do are nonetheless striking.

Whatever the reason, it does not take long for the child to leave the two-part sentence stage behind, and begin to understand and to produce sentences which contain three or four main parts. A sentence such as *Kick ball* at age 2 contains just a 'Verb' *kick* and an 'Object' *ball*. After a while, such sentences are said with a 'Subject' expressed also, such as *Man kick ball* or *Him kick ball*. Later still, a fourth part may be added (an 'Adverbial'), expressing the time, place, or manner of the action: *Man kick ball now*, *Man kick ball there*, *Man kick ball hard*.

This is just one type of sentence, of course. Another type at age 2 might be *Man sad* (meaning 'the man is sad'). This might build up into *Man be sad*, and then other parts might be added, as above – *Man be sad now*.

At the same time as children develop their ability to produce statements, they learn to ask questions and give commands. We've already seen the way in which early questions are formed (p. 96). During the third year, questions become more complex, as they too become longer. *Where daddy going?* at age 2 can be compared to *Where will you put my presents in the morning?*. The first has only three parts (*where* + *daddy* + *going*); the second has five (*where* + *you* + *will-put* + *my-presents* + *in-the-morning*). Commands become more sophisticated too. *Push car* at age 2 should be compared to *Push the car in the garage now* at age 3.

You'll have noticed that many of these sentences have a strange, abrupt appearance. They resemble the style of adult telegrams. *Send money urgently. Daddy arrives tomorrow airport.* Children's speech at around age 2 has often been called 'telegrammatic' or 'telegraphic'. By age 3, it has lost its telegrammatic character. The 'little words', such as *is*, *in*, *the* and *do*, begin to make their presence felt. At first, a sentence might consist only of the 'main' words, such as *man kick ball*. Then the different parts 'fill out', to produce sentences which sound much more correct and adult: *The man is kicking that ball.*

Of course, it doesn't happen overnight. There are many steps between the telegrammatic and the mature patterns. Here are some sentences taken from children who are on their way to the mature style, but who haven't reached it yet:

My cat eating a mouse. (The verb is not yet fully developed.)
He do falling over. (Again, the verb is incorrect.)
Daddy give me big kiss. (The verb is wrong, and a word like *a*
should be used in front of *big kiss*.)

Sometimes, the first sign of words like *the* or *a* emerging is a noise which hardly sounds like a word at all. *Kick ball*, says the child; and then, it comes out as *kick (brief noise) ball*. The noise might sound like 'uh', very short and quiet. You wouldn't be able to say what word it was: it might be *the*, *a*, or even *my* or *that*. It's as if children know that there should be *some* word between *kick* and *ball*, but they're not sure what – so they make an unclear noise, to be on the safe side. I've done a very similar thing when faced with a French noun, and not known whether to say *le* or *la* before it: I produce a vowel which is neither one thing nor the other and hope no one will notice.

You can see from these examples that children's sentences are getting more complex in the third year. Moreover, two things are happening at once. They are adding more parts to the simple structures present at age 2. And they are making each part more complex at the same time. Here's a diagram to explain this relationship. The first sentence is getting more complex because extra main parts are being added. The second sentence is based on the first, but now other words have been added to each part.

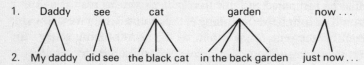

1.   Daddy   see   cat   garden   now . . .
2.   My daddy did see the black cat in the back garden just now . . .

Any one of these parts can become very complex indeed. A phrase such as *the black cat* can be made even bigger, by adding extra words to it:

> the black cat
> the big black cat
> the three big black cats
> the three big black cats with long tails.

You and I can say this sort of thing. Children have to learn to do so. They begin this task in their third year.

However, when children start to fill out their sentence parts in this way, you'll find that they don't do the whole job at once. Some parts get filled out before others. Here's a basic sentence:

> Dog chase cat.

Now, imagine a 2-year-old who has learned a few adjectives, such as *black* and *big*. Which of the following three possibilities will happen first? Will the adjective be added to the 'Subject' of the sentence?

> Black dog chase cat

Or will it be added to the 'Object' of the sentence?

> Dog chase black cat

Or will both come at about the same time?

> Black dog chase black cat.

Most people think that the third answer is correct. Once you've learned to use adjectives, you can use them wherever you like, they reason. In fact, this doesn't happen very much. A far more usual development is for adjectives to be used in one part of the sentence before they're used in another. Of the above three, it is the second possibility which is normally the earliest to emerge. The first possibility turns up later – sometimes weeks or months later.

It's not just adjectives. It's normal for extra words to get into a sentence through the back door, turning up after the verb towards the end of the sentence. Far fewer extra words turn up before the verb, at the beginning of a sentence. You'll often hear such sentences as:

The cowboy chased the big fat indian in a hat.

But you won't hear many sentences such as:

A big fat indian in a hat chased the cowboy.

Why not? Partly because it's not usual to put lots of specific words at the beginning of a sentence in adult English. Once we've introduced a topic, we tend to refer back to it quite briefly, leaving all the interesting new details until later in the sentence. The first sentence in a story might be:

The tall handsome cowboy rode in to town.

But later sentences will not repeat this long phrase. The story will continue:

He was looking for the sheriff.

and not

The tall handsome cowboy was looking for the sheriff.

Over half of the sentences we say in everyday conversation have just a single word before the verb – a pronoun, such as *he*, *I* or *you*. If we measured adult sentences with a ruler, we would find in most cases that the length before the verb was short and the length after the verb was long. Look at these, for instance:

The man kicked the ball into the back garden.
_____   _____

We asked Mary to come to see us next week.
_____   _____

A sentence which is constructed the other way round sounds very unwieldy and formal, and is much more difficult to understand:

> That Mary should come to see us next week is fine.

It's not surprising then that children should follow this pattern too.

Word endings

The development of word endings is one of the most noticeable features of the third year. Some endings are already in evidence before two. A few verbs will have the *-ing* ending (as in *Him running*) and a few nouns will have the *-s* ending which makes the difference between singular and plural (as in *boy/boys*). But most of the endings start to appear in the third year.

Not that there are very many to be learned in English. English children have an advantage over French, German or Finnish children in this respect – though it's only a temporary advantage, for they have to sort out the greater complications of English word order instead! In fact, apart from the two just mentioned, there are only a handful of other endings:

the verb ending which expresses distant past time – usually *-ed*, as in *I jumped*, but there are many irregular forms, such as *saw* or *went* (as we've seen in Chapter 1);

another verb ending, which helps to express recent past time – also usually *-ed* (as in *I've asked*), but here too there are many irregular forms, such as *taken* and *gone*;

the *-s* verb ending which is used in the present tense to show that the Subject of the sentence is singular, as in *he walks* or *the lady runs* – other forms of the verb don't have this ending (*I walk*, *you walk*, and so on);

several verbs can be shortened, and attach themselves to the Subject of a sentence, as in *he's coming* (short for *is*), *they've gone* (short for *have*), and *she'd find* (short for *would*);

not can be shortened to *-n't* and attached to a verb, as in *isn't* and *wouldn't*;

many nouns can add *-'s* or *-s'* to express such meanings as possession – as in *the man's hat* and *the cat's dish*;

many adjectives can add *-er* and *-est* to express different kinds of comparison, as in *he's bigger* and *he's biggest*.

If these endings were all used in a nice and regular way, children would have few problems in learning them. But none of them is straightforward. English is cluttered with different types of nouns, verbs and adjectives, some of which take the usual endings, some take exceptional endings, and some take no endings at all.

Children have got to sort out several complicated rules. Take the *-ing* ending, for instance, which is the first to be thoroughly learned. This is used on most verbs, to express the duration of an action, but it mustn't be used on such verbs as *know* and *see*, which talk about sensations and mental states. You can't usually say *the man is knowing* or *the girl is seeing*; and if you say *the boy is smelling*, it means something different from what you expected! Children in fact do very well with this ending and rarely get it wrong. Errors such as *the man is seeing his coat* are not at all common.

By contrast, the plural ending on nouns gives rise to many errors, because irregular forms are so common – *men*, *mice*, *geese*, and so on. You'll notice an interesting development here with many children. To begin with, they may actually produce these irregular forms correctly, saying such things as *see the geese* and *three blind mice*. But don't be fooled. They aren't really budding grammarians. They haven't learned the meaning of 'plural' at this stage; they've simply picked up the irregular forms from somewhere and begun to use them 'off by heart'. You can tell this because they will say *mice* while pointing to just one mouse, or they may even say *a mice*.

The first real sign that they know what plural means comes later. They then try out the plural endings on these words, producing such forms as *mices* and *mouses*. If you weren't expecting this, you might feel disappointed when this happens – as if the child had taken a step backwards in language learning. But don't be depressed. On the contrary, when children first start adding the normal endings on to these nouns, it's a major step forward. It's one of the clearest signs that they are learning the rules of grammar for themselves, and not just parroting what they hear around them. They're getting the rules wrong as they try them out, but this is only natural. There'll be a long period of trial and error, until they sort everything out. You'll find that by the middle of the fourth year most of the errors have disappeared.

Similar patterns of development are found with the other word endings. Here are some typical third-year errors:

You bettern't do that.	My hand's the biggest than Ben's.
It just got brokened.	That's the mans's car.
That's much more better.	My sore's worser now.

Lucy: Squeak, squeak – that's what mouses does.
Mother: That's what *mice* do.
Lucy: What do mices does?

Vocabulary

Nobody's ever been able to arrive at an accurate estimate of a child's spoken vocabulary in the third year. It would be a real labour of love, involving a vast team of tape recorders and transcribers. Just think of how many samples you'd have to take to make sure you'd caught most of the words. One of the samples would have to be in December, to catch all the Christmassy words. Another would have to be at holiday time to catch all the seaside words. Then there are Easter bunnies, birthdays, television programmes, and a thousand other experiences which all generate their own vocabulary. It would take a lot of time, and a lot of money, to find out what goes on. Time, there is, in our unemployed age; money, there isn't.

Those who have tried to study vocabulary in the third year report a real spurt in the second half of the year. One report mentions 500 words by $2\frac{1}{2}$, and 1,000 words by 3, but this is certainly an underestimate for many children. It also doesn't allow for the way in which words come to be *used* during this year. For a 2-year-old, the word *dog* refers to the animal 'dog', and to little else – unless the word comes to be 'over-extended' (see p. 72) to a few other animals. By 3, many words have begun to take on several meanings.

This is the normal state of affairs in language. Most words in

English have more than one meaning, as is immediately obvious if you look at the pages of a dictionary. All the different senses are listed there. *Table* can mean a piece of furniture, the food served at a meal (*he keeps a good table*), a negotiating session (*the peace table*), a list of figures (*Table 1*), and a piece of flat high ground (*Table Mountain*). Then there are all the idioms which use the word, such as *it's on the table* (= 'it's been put forward for discussion'), *turn the tables* (= 'to cause fortunes to be reversed'), or *put your cards on the table* (= 'to divulge your intentions'). To learn vocabulary is to learn all of this, or at least the commonest meanings.

Most of the senses of *table* are for adults only, of course. But there are many words that 3-year-olds are likely to meet where meanings need to be distinguished.

funny 'amusing' or 'strange',
call 'shout', 'visit' or 'telephone',
leave 'go away' or 'let something stay as it is',
plug 'object in a wash-basin' (which you're allowed to touch) or 'object in the wall' (which you're not),
side 'a part of your body', 'one surface of a piece of paper', or 'a team of people',
low 'near the ground' or 'not loud'.

Now imagine two 2½-year-old children. Both have learned these six words, but one child has learned only one sense per word, whereas the other child has learned all the senses of each word. If you just counted the words, the two children would come out the same. But if you counted the meanings, the second child would have a total of 14 different uses, compared with the first child's six. That's why it's so important to write down the meaning of a word when you're keeping a diary (see p. 104). If you don't, you'll miss this very important feature of a child's development in the third year.

But there's another big feature of vocabulary learning which becomes quite noticeable during this year. You'll notice at around 2½ that they start asking lots of questions about the names of things. 'What's that called?', 'What's that?' Parents cope quite well with the first hundred or so questions – not quite so well with the next 8,000! Nor do they cope so well with some of the follow-up questions which arise, as in this dialogue:

Jamie (2;8): What's that, mummy?
Mother: That's a jackdaw.
Jamie: Why is it a jackdaw?
Mother (*pause, then lamely*): Because that's its name, darling.

Some *why* questions can carry on for ages.

This period of intense questioning has an important purpose. It's a way in which children can find out how words relate to each other. Adults do the same thing when they're learning a new vocabulary. If you've ever sat in an evening class looking blankly at a vast number of house plants, or at the bits of a car engine, you'll have a sense of the problem facing the child. As you try to sort out what's what, you ask all kinds of questions. Here are some heard at one such class; but I'll leave out the crucial words, which could be the names of plants, bits of engine, or anything:

Q: What's that? Is that a —?
A: No, look, you're mixing it up with —. It's much smaller, see?
Q: Well what about this, then? Is that a —too?
A: No, that's a —. It's very similar in shape, but the colour's not quite the same.

Children at this age don't have the language to enter into conversations like this, but the same kind of reasoning is involved. When they meet a new word, they have to relate it to the words they already know, to work out when you should use one word and not the other. Here are some conversations to show how it's done:

Child: Ooh look, mummy, a horse.
Mother: That's not a horse, it's a zebra. See, it's got stripes.
Child: Can I ride on that zebra?

Child: I got a yellow car.
Mother: That's an *orange* car. Look, there's a yellow one. They're different, aren't they?

Child: Can I have one of those apples?
Mother: They're peaches, not apples.
Child: Can I have one?
Mother: You might not like them (*gives one*).
Child: It's all furry (*examines it, then bites*). Yuk.

In each case, the new word is immediately put alongside the familiar word, and a contrast is drawn between the two. In the first two cases, the mother makes the contrast; in the third case, the child does.

Of course, a child won't necessarily get a distinction right after hearing it only once. Some differences in meaning are very subtle and take a long time to be acquired. The words which express dimensions, for example, are quite awkward – words such as *big*, *little*, *wide*, *narrow*, *fat*, and *thin*. The first two to appear are usually *big* and *little* (or some similar word, such as *small* or *wee*). Next are such pairs as *long/short* and *high/low*, which are much more specific than *big/small*. Later still, during the fourth year, are such pairs as *thick/thin* and *deep/shallow*.

But there are all kinds of traps in store for the language-learning child. What's the difference between *big* and *tall*, for instance? Or *little* and *short*? The child has to learn that shops can be *big* but not *tall*, but buildings can be either *big* or *tall*. *Look at that tall building* is acceptable English. *Look at that tall shop* is odd. Moreover, one of the words seems to be more widely used than the other. We say (if we've gone metric) that a man is *two metres tall*, but if we compare him to someone who is only one metre in size, we don't say the other person is *one metre short*. We still use the word *tall* and say *one metre tall*. Similarly we say (if we haven't gone metric yet) that a swimming pool is *nine feet deep* at the deep end and *three feet deep* at the shallow end, not *three feet shallow*. You'll hear many errors in what children say, as they try to sort out these distinctions.

Sometimes it is the objects themselves in the outside world which are unclear. Imagine the kind of glass you drink out of. Now imagine it getting taller. At what point would you stop calling it a *glass* and start calling it a *vase* or an *ornament*? Or imagine it getting wider. At what point would it stop being a glass and start being a *bowl* or a *dish*? The answer isn't obvious and perhaps there is no answer. Adults too are sometimes uncertain whether to call an object by one name or another. The boundary between objects is not always clear, and it may not be obvious which word to use. The same applies to colours. Is an object *green* or *blue?* It might be neither. It might be *greeny-blue*, or *bluey-green*, or some other uncertain shade.

Progress everywhere

There's so much going on in grammar and vocabulary in the third year that you might forget to notice that the sounds of the language are developing as well. By three, children have begun to use almost all their vowels, and they have about twice as many consonants in use as they did at two years. They are using the sounds in longer words, too. Words of three syllables can be heard, such as *elephant* and *telephone*. And they are beginning to alter the way they emphasize the words in a sentence to bring out the meaning. *You got a little crocodile, I got a big one* said one 3-year-old, and she made the words *little* and *big* really stand out. *I made a big big big snowball* said another, saying each adjective loud and long.

Nor should you forget the great progress the child is making in 'conversational skills' during this period. Here are two extracts from conversations recorded by Paul Fletcher, who carried out a diary study of a child between 2 and 4. The first recording was made when the child was 2;4. It shows a lot of typical 2-year-old repetitive speech, with the child apparently talking to herself much of the time as she plays. The conversation works well enough, but it is erratic and disjointed.

Child: Me want – Look! Balls. You like those balls?
Mother: Yes.
Child: Ball. Kick. Kick. Daddy kick.
Mother: That's right, you have to kick it, don't you.
Child: Mmm. Um. Um. Kick hard. Only kick hard . . . Our play that. On floor. Our play that on floor. Now. Our play that. On floor. Our play that on floor. No that. Now.
Mother: All right.
Child: Mummy, come on floor me.

Mother: Yes.
Child: You tip those out.
Mother: Mmm. All right.

By contrast, the conversation at 3 is a real dialogue, or rather, argument, in this extract! – with both parties much more involved in what each is saying.

Child: Hester be fast asleep, mummy.
Mother: She was tired.
Child: And why did her have two sweets, mummy?
Mother: Because you each had two, that's why. She had the same as you. Ooh dear, now what?
Child: Daddy didn't give me two in the end.
Mother: Yes, he did.
Child: He didn't.
Mother: He did.
Child: Look, he given one to – two to Hester, and two to us.
Mother: Yes, that's right.
Child: Why did he give?
Mother: Because there were six sweets. That's two each.

To conclude

The third year is a period of massive development and consolidation of language skills. At two, children are linguistic toddlers. At three, they're linguistic analysts, full of questions and arguments. They say much more, and they say it with impressive fluency and accuracy. There are still lots of errors to be sorted out, of course, and there are large areas of language waiting to be explored. But there's plenty of time, before they have to survive the new language worlds of playgroup and school.

Feature 11 | What time is it?

Long before children learn to tell the time on a clock, they learn to talk about time in their sentences. There are few other topics in language acquisition which are more important than this – or more complicated.

How do adults talk about time? Mainly by changing the form of the verb to make different 'tenses'. For instance, when you say *I see a car*, this form of the verb (the 'present tense') tells the listener that you're seeing the object while you're speaking. On the other hand, if you said *I saw a car*, the different verb-form (the 'past tense') would convey that the car isn't there any more. The usual past tense ending in English is *-ed* (*I walked/jumped/asked . . .*), but there are over 200 irregular past tenses (*I saw/went/took . . .*), which always cause problems of language learning.

To express other times, English has a small set of verbs which are used with the main verb in the sentence. These are known as 'auxiliary' verbs. Some of these verbs are used to express future time:

> I will see I shall see
> I'm going to see I'm about to see.

Other kinds of past time use the auxiliary verbs *have* and *did*, as in *I have seen*, *I had seen*, and *Did you go?*. Also, important differences can be made by adding various time expressions. For instance, if you say *I'm writing to John*, you're doing the action as you speak; whereas if you say *I'm writing to John tomorrow*, you haven't begun the action yet. There are hundreds of these time expressions in a language, such as *soon*, *next week*, *then*, *yesterday*, and *in a year's time*.

How do children set about mastering this complex system of expression? At the earliest stage, there is only the present tense form, which is used to express past and future time, as well as present. Here are some examples, where the present tense clearly refers to past time.

(*Michael falls down*)
Mother: What's the matter?
Michael (1;6): I fall down.

(*Jane knocks her bricks over*)
Jane (1;8): Push over.

Also, during the second year, children learn to emphasize the duration of an action, using the 'continuous' or 'progressive' form of the verb. This is signalled by the use of the *-ing* ending, as in *Him running* and *Man sweeping*. A little later, and the auxiliary verb *be* is also used: *Him is running*, *Man be sweeping*.

Around 2, there are the first signs of the past tense, using the *-ed* ending, which is used for many of the irregular verbs as well:

I swallowed it.	Him falled over.
Daddy pushed me.	It all wiped up now.
We eated it all up.	You drinked it.

Look out for which verbs are the earliest to take the past tense ending. In one study, it was found that the verbs which are first used in this way are typically those which express a clear action with a definite end point – such as the above. You can see when something has been swallowed, wiped up, or drunk. Verbs like *know*, *stay*, *have*, and *see*, where the action is less obvious, are not put into the past tense at this stage.

During the first half of the third year, there are several developments in the verb. Children start using such auxiliaries as *do*, *have*, *can*, and *will*. *Have* is especially important for the expression of time, as it helps to form the so-called 'perfect' tense – *he's finished*, *it's stopped*, *I've seen him*, and so on. The verb *got* is particularly common with this form, as in *I've got a car*, *Mummy's got one*. There were hints of this pattern in the second year, with such sentences as *him gone* and *that broken*, but there wouldn't have been an auxiliary verb then.

The difference in meaning between the past tense form and the perfect tense form is important. If you say *He's fallen over*, the event has probably just happened – it's *recent* past time. But if you say *He fell over*, the event could have happened some time ago –

the past time is more *remote*. You can say *He fell over a year ago*, but you can't easily say *He's fallen over a year ago*.

In the following exchange, Lucy shows she can understand the difference between past tense and perfect tense, but she isn't producing the contrast in her speech.

Lucy: He throwed it on the floor again.
Mother (*wanting to correct the error*): He *threw* it on the floor, did he?
Lucy: Yes, but he only *just* throwed it on the floor.

When Lucy hears her mother's correction she interprets it as a past tense, as if mother is saying the action happened some time ago. She therefore brings in extra words to stress that the action is recent, but she still uses the past tense form, instead of the correct *he's only just thrown*.

Lucy was 4 when she said this. By 4;3 she was beginning to use *have* quite regularly in her speech, though this was quite late for a British child. In Britain, the form is common by 3;6. In America, however, the pattern is found to emerge later, presumably because American speakers prefer such usages as *I just ate*, whereas British people prefer *I've just eaten*.

Note that in such phrases as *he's falling* and *he's fallen*, the *'s* is short for *is* in the first case and *has* in the second. This can be a source of great confusion. Witness the errors made by this 3-year-old:

Is it got a new tyre?	He is fallen over.
Why is daddy gone out?	She has running away.

Some of the most fascinating errors made by children during their third year are of this kind. They arise because it takes a long time to sort out the complicated grammar of auxiliary verbs and tense forms in the language. Look at these lovely errors, taken from various research studies, all from the first half of the third year:

Whose is that is?	I'm want some dinner.
What did you did?	That's makes a truck.
Did you came home?	I did fell.
What did you bought?	The plant didn't cried.

Working out why these errors take place has kept several language acquisition scholars very busy for some time.

Around 4, children come to express more complex meanings, using other time words and phrases. Here are some of Lucy's sentences at 4;2:

I like it so much 'cos I haven't seen you wore it *for a long time.*
I done some number drawings *today.*
That flower has grown with the rain *yesterday.*
Chloe's *just* went upstairs to catch mouses.

But there are still many errors to be sorted out:

I didn't saw him go in that little bus.
Why haven't you gave me a banana?
I looked and see it.
I didn't thought you were going to wash it today.
She was wears it when she was a little girl, and she wears it
   now too.
If I went to the party today, I not feel well. (= 'I wouldn't
   have felt well')

By 4;6, Lucy is trying out several more advanced auxiliary verbs, but most are wrong:

   I *would* wish they *would* let me be the farmer.
   Daddy, please *may* you jump me high?
   I keep my hanky in my bag like you *used to* did.

And there is this remarkable triple-auxiliary sequence:

I might sit here till I've drinked this, or it *might have been*
   gone. (that is, it might be gone already)

Some of these forms won't be fully mastered until age 7 or 8, and learning all the meanings of these forms can take until around 10 years of age. Learning to tell the time on a clock is much easier.

Feature 12 | You, me and the others

Language gone mad! That must surely be the verdict of any child who meets words like *I*, *me*, and *you* for the first time – the 'pronouns'. Put yourself in their shoes. What would you be thinking, on your first close encounter with linguistic situations like these?

> Daddy says 'Show me', and *me* means Daddy.
> Mummy says 'Show me', and *me* means Mummy.
> I say 'Show me', and *me* means me.

Or this:

Daddy says 'Show me', and *me* means Daddy.
Daddy says 'I know', and *I* means Daddy.
Mummy says 'You go', and *you* means Daddy.
Grandma tells Mummy 'He's outside', and *he* means Daddy.
Grandma tells Mummy 'He's outside', and *he* means the milkman.

How can a sensible person be expected to learn a language if there are words which change their meaning all the time? Oh for the days when *dog* meant 'dog' and that was all there was to it!

Children get to grips with pronouns in the third year. The amazing thing is that, despite the complexity, they do so well. Faced with a situation where *me* and *you* change their meaning depending on who is talking, you might expect that they would always be mixing them up – saying *you* instead of *me*, and vice versa. This is in fact quite rare.

In 1982, Shulamuth Chiat published a study of a child who did reverse his pronouns in this way. Matthew was 2;4 at the time. She first of all tested his comprehension of pronouns by asking him to carry out certain actions: 'Put this ring on my finger', 'Put this ring on your finger', 'Where are my eyes?', 'Where are your eyes?', and so on. Matthew hardly ever made a mistake. He certainly understood the difference between the 'first person' pronouns (*I*, *me*, *my*) and the 'second person' pronouns (*you*, *your*).

But when Matthew spoke, the situation was very different, as these examples show:

Shula (the researcher): What will happen if you cut my hair?
Matthew: I'll cry.
Shula: Who'll cry?
Matthew: Shula.

In this example, he used *I* to mean 'you'. In the next, he used *you* to mean 'I':

Shula: I don't think you'd better snip your hair off.
Matthew: What will happen?
Shula: What will happen?
Matthew: You'll cry.
Shula: Who'll cry?
Matthew: Matthew.

He didn't do this all the time. In fact, the majority of his pronouns were used correctly. He hardly ever had trouble with the *we/our* forms, or with the 'third person' forms (*he*, *him*, *his*, *her*, and so on). And he often got the first person singular form right. In one recording session, he correctly used 173 pronouns to refer to himself but reversed another 44. However, in the same session, he had much more difficulty with the *you* forms: he got only five of these right, and reversed 71.

Sometimes, he used both a correct and an incorrect form in the same sentence. On one occasion, he approached Shula and said:

I'm gonna chop my hair off with these

where the situation made it clear that the first pronoun was referring (correctly) to Matthew, and the second (incorrectly) to Shula.

But Matthew is the exception not the rule. Most children who have had their pronouns studied seem to make very few errors of this kind. Far more common are such patterns as the following.

1. They often avoid pronouns altogether, replacing them with the name of the person involved.

John (*taking hold of daddy's hand*): Daddy come with me.

Mother: Who put this in here?
Micky (*laughing*): Micky did it.
Mother: Well, Micky shouldn't!

This usage is not very surprising, especially as adults do tend to talk to children in a similar style, as this example in fact shows. *Give it to mummy*, mummy might say, rather than *Give it to me*. *Johnny come for a walk with daddy?*, daddy might say, talking to Johnny, instead of using the more normal *you*.

2. Children frequently mix up the Subject and Object forms of a pronoun. In English, we say *I*, *he*, *she*, *we*, and *they* at the beginning of a sentence, and *me*, *him*, *her*, *us*, and *them* in other places. *He saw her. I sat next to him.* Children have trouble with this distinction. It doesn't convey any difference of meaning. There's no reason for it, except – that's the way English is. Not surprisingly, then, it takes children a while to work out what goes where. Usually they replace the Subject forms by the Object forms:

> Him did it.
> Her gave me one.
> Them's all gone now.

But you'll sometimes hear the error go in the other direction:

> Let she do it.
> I gonna push they over.

Mother: Who did it?
Child: He.

And you'll often find inconsistency:

> She likes to do that, her do.

3. Another common pattern of error is to mix up these pronouns with those which express possession. Here, English makes

another awkward distinction. We say *my car*, but *the car is mine*; *your car*, but *the car is yours*; and so on. Some words add an *-s* (*yours*, *ours*, *theirs*, *hers*), some don't (*mine*), and some have already got an *-s* (*his*, *its*). It's a messy situation which foreigners take ages to learn, so don't be surprised to find such muddles as these:

> This is him's car. | I can see she's bed.
> Mys want to come in. | My finished now.

It takes children the best part of two years to work out all the complexities of the English pronoun system. But the effort is well worth while. There are few words which will be used more frequently throughout the rest of their linguistic lives.

Feature 13 | Saying no

Babies are usually quite good at letting their parents know that they *don't* want something to happen. The furious howl which accompanies a wet flannel placed against a sticky face leaves no doubt in anyone's mind about the child's ability to communicate 'no'. But what happens later?

Young children rely a great deal on negative gestures. They learn to shake their heads, frown, and turn away. During the second year, they learn some linguistic ways of saying no as well. The gestures are never replaced, though. Adults have every right to shake their heads and frown if they want to.

1. The first stage is the use of a negative word – usually *no* or *not*. It may not even be a clear word, but more a negative noise, such as *n-n-n*. Some children use a quite different word to express negative meaning, such as *gone* or *bye*. *Gone bed, gone bed*, said one child, as she was carried reluctantly towards her cot.

2. When *no* comes to be used, it is quickly combined with other words at the two-word stage of development (see p. 76). You'll hear such sentences as:

> No sit.
> No fall down.
> Running no.
> Not wipe it.

The negative word is found at the beginning or at the end of the sentence. It doesn't occur inside. You won't hear sentences such as *Me no go* at this stage.

In one of the first studies of this topic, Lois Bloom found that these early negative sentences expressed several kinds of meaning. One meaning is 'something doesn't exist', 'something isn't in its usual place', as when a child might say *No car* while looking at an empty garage. A second meaning is that of rejection, as when a child says *No drink juice*, pushing a cup away. A third meaning is one of denial, as when *Not my coat* is said, pointing to someone else's coat.

3. As sentences get longer, negative words come to be used within sentences, as well as at the beginnings or ends. Most of this development takes place in the third year. These examples are all from children in the first half of this year:

> You no do that. I no want to go bed.
> Mummy not got it

At about the same time, verbs such as *can't*, *don't*, and *won't* begin to appear:

> Me can't do that. I don't know. Don't do that.
> Her won't sit down properly.

For many children, *can't* and *won't* appear some time before they say *can* and *will*! What does *that* tell us, I wonder?

4. The next stage is for the negative words and endings inside the sentence to become more accurately used. *Not* replaces *no*, and *n't* is used with more auxiliary verbs (see p. 118):

> She isn't going. You've not got one.

But there are still errors. In particular, you'll notice that children are very ready to use 'double negatives', such as:

> She can't not get up. Nobody don't like to go in.

Don't look at these in a mathematical or logical way. The two negatives don't 'cancel out' and make a positive. To the child, two negatives make a more emphatic negative! Even three negatives can be heard together, at times.

5. There are a few other rules to be learned before the art of saying no is completely mastered, but these are not acquired until much later. There's the rule which makes us say *I've got some* and *I've not got any* – rather than *I've got any* and *I've not got some*. There's the rule which says that with such words as *hardly* and

scarcely you don't use a negative word because these words are negative in meaning already – *I hardly spoke to him* rather than *I didn't hardly speak to him* (though this pattern is in fact used in some dialects).

6. Lastly, there's the important skill to be learned of saying no without saying no. Parents are particularly good at this, when talking to children in their fourth year or later. *Can I have a biscuit?*, asks the child. *It'll be tea time in a little while* says mother, a negative sentence if ever there was one, but containing no negative word at all. Children don't quite know how to take these, when they first hear them:

Child: Can I have a biscuit, mummy?
Mother: You've just had one.
(*Pause.*)
Child: Yes, but can I have one now?
Mother: No, I just told you, you've just had one.

But they soon learn. Mother spells out the negative meaning in her second reply and emphasizes it with a sharp tone of voice as well. By 5, children have become quite skilled at reading between the lines of an adult sentence. Which is just as well, for they'll get plenty of opportunity to use this skill in school.

Feature 14 | Grammatical bits and pieces

Do children learn the different word endings of English in a particular order? This was one of the first questions to be studied by child language researchers in the 1960s. The answer seems to be yes.

Roger Brown published a detailed study of the way in which three American children learned to use word endings over a period of time. The first two were dubbed Adam and Eve; the third was called Sarah. Eve was 1;6 at the beginning of the study; the others were 2;3. But all three were at roughly the same linguistic stage of development. Recordings were systematically made every week or so – for a year, in Eve's case, and for another four years, for Adam and Sarah.

In addition to the main word endings, Brown included a study of some of the important 'grammatical words' of English – they're such words as *the*, *is* and *in*, which help a sentence to hang together.

He found that these items were learned in the following order.

1. The -*ing* ending on verbs, as in *He's running*.
2. The preposition *in*, as in *It's in the box*.
3. The preposition *on*, as in *It's on the table*.
4. The regular plural ending, -*s*, as in *cats and dogs*.
5. The irregular past tense form, such as *went*.
6. The -*s* ending on nouns, which expresses possession, as in *the boy's car*.
7. The full form of the verb *to be*, when it is the only verb in a sentence, as in *Are they there?*, *Is he ready?*
8. The definite and indefinite articles, *the* and *a*.
9. The regular past tense ending, -*ed*, as in *He jumped*.
10. The regular ending for the 3rd person form of the verb, in the present tense, -*s*, as in *he walks*.
11. The irregular ending for the 3rd person form, as in *he has* or *he does*.

12. The full form of the verb *to be*, when it is an auxiliary verb in a sentence, as in *Are they running?*
13. The shortened form of the verb *to be*, when it is the only verb in a sentence, as in *He's ready*, *They're there.*
14. The shortened form of the verb *to be*, when it is an auxiliary verb in a sentence, as in *They're coming*, *He's going.*

There were a few small variations between the three children, but on the whole the way in which each one learned these forms was very consistent. Moreover, since then, several investigators have looked at other children and found a similar order of acquisition.

Finding out the order of acquisition is one thing. Working out *why* children acquire the items in this order is quite another. Why should *in* be acquired before *on*? Why should the plural ending on nouns be acquired before the possessive ending? The simple answer would be that children learn first the item that occurs most frequently in the language they hear around them. But it turns out not to be so simple.

The reason seems more to do with the complexity of the items – the kind of job they do in a sentence and the meaning that they express. *-ing* is a nice simple ending, expressing a single meaning ('continuity', or 'duration'). *-s* is more complicated: it has a single meaning ('more than one'), but it appears in many forms: it sounds different in *cats*, *dogs*, and *horses*, and there are many irregular plurals (*mice*, *geese*, and so on). The verb *to be* is more complex still. It expresses both singular/plural *and* present/past time – *is/are* and *is/was*, for example.

However, it isn't easy to work out why one of these items is more or less complex than another. Child language researchers have mixed feelings about what is going on. But the facts about the order of emergence are plain enough, so you should find the same thing in your child too. *-ing* first? *In* before *on*? Roger Brown's checklist can keep you busy for months.

'Isn't he tall! Why, only a month ago he was ...' Measuring a child's height is a nice simple way of checking that everything is going according to plan. Weight is another. Could there be a nice simple way of checking that language development is going according to plan?

Probably not. Language has too many features which develop at different rates and times. Sounds don't develop in the same way as words. And grammar contains a thousand different features – pronouns, verbs, word order ... – each of which has its own pattern of growth.

But still ... Perhaps if we measured how long a sentence is? Would we then have a clear index of development? Several investigators have thought so and worked out ways to do it. The most famous measuring-rod for sentences was devised by Roger Brown. He called his measure the 'Mean Length of Utterance' MLU, for short. It's been widely used in studies of child language and it's very helpful in showing how sentences gradually get longer in the early years.

For older children, such measures are less helpful. There comes a point when sentences become more complicated inside without necessarily getting longer. You can have two sentences of exactly the same length, but one can be much more complex than the other. Compare *The man rang the bell and went away* and *The man who rang the bell has gone*. Both are eight words, each more or less the same length; but the second sentence is much more difficult to learn than the first – and would be acquired by children at a much later age.

You also have to decide which units to count. Do you count the number of words in a sentence, or the number of syllables, or the number of word-parts (such as *-ing*, *un-* and *-ness*)? Roger Brown chose the last of these, but this involves quite a technical procedure. In the approach below, I'll be counting the number of words.

If you decide to measure your child's sentence length it's usual to work this out using a sample of a fixed length. This will make it easier to compare the score you obtain on one occasion with the score you obtain on another. You can then also compare the scores of different children more easily. The usual size of sample is 100 sentences. But don't start yet. There are a few things you should bear in mind before you begin to count the number of words in each sentence.

1. You need to make a recording of a good stretch of the child's spontaneous speech. About 10 or 15 minutes will do. Make sure it's a natural, comfortable play situation. Try to say things that you would usually say in such a situation. But don't talk too much, in the hope that this will make children say more. They won't. Too much parentspeak often has the reverse effect.

2. After you've made the recording, you need to transcribe the sentences. It'll take a bit of time, and you may have to listen to some sentences several times to be sure you've written them down correctly. If you can't understand a sentence, because it's unintelligible, or because it's obscured by some passing noise, leave it out.

3. Don't bother with the first few sentences of the recording. These probably won't be very typical, as both you and the child will be settling down, and you're likely to be using special sentences – greeting, discussing what to play, and so on. If you can't see an obvious place to start, start at the top of the second page of your transcription.

4. Write each sentence on a separate line. This will make it easier to count them up later. But beware. It's sometimes difficult to decide where one sentence stops and the next starts. You have to listen carefully to the melody and rhythm of each utterance, and note the pauses which separate them. With very young children, words can be so jammed together that it's almost impossible to know whether you're dealing with one sentence, or two, or more. The same applies to older children when they start linking sentences with *and* (see p. 143). If you can't decide, you'd better leave the utterance out of your count. It won't make any difference to the final score.

5. If children repeat a sentence several times, you can count each repetition as a new sentence.

6. Don't forget to include the short sentences in your count – such as *no*, *m*, *sorry*, *ta*. Remember that even emotional noises, such as *oh* and *coo*, can be used as sentences.

7. When you're counting the number of words in each sentence, you can ignore any hesitation noises (such as *er*) and any groups of stammered words count as one (for example, *he he he went home* contains three words).

8. Take care that you write a compound word down as a single unit, otherwise you might count it as two words. A *blackbird* is not the same thing as a *black bird*. Sometimes, you might be unsure whether to write something down as one word or two. Is it *washing machine* or *washing-machine*? In such cases, count as one word. This way you won't run the risk of overestimating the child's sentence length.

That's all. Here's a sample which I've worked out, to show you how it's done.

Me got that.	Him go on there.
Where you going now?	No.
Me come.	Not me.
Me come.	You do it.
Put it down there.	That big one.

The total number of words is 28. The total number of sentences is 10. Therefore the mean number of words per sentence is 2·8.

If you want to measure the sentence length of your own child, there are specially printed pages available in Appendix 2 (p. 225).

5 | The Pre-school Years

At around age 3 there is a dramatic change in children's language. If any age has to be called a linguistic milestone, it has to be this. And yet it's all due to one of the smallest words: *and*.

If you look out for the word *and* in your child's speech, you'll probably first notice it towards the middle of the third year. It's used in short phrases, such as *mummy and daddy*, and is often pronounced in a clipped way, as *'n*. Here are a few sentences using *and* produced by Lucy at 2;9:

> That's nice and dirty now.
> I don't want toys and things on there.
> Steven and Susie be hiding.
> And me.

But Lucy quickly learned that *and* is a more powerful word than that. Once you've learned it, you can use it to join three words or four – or four hundred! Here, just before 3, she launches herself into a monologue that would have lasted for ever, if mother hadn't intervened. She's trying to decide what toy to take to bed with her.

Lucy: And I want teddy, and that teddy, and my dolly, and
   Mister Happy, and that one, and –
Mother: Hey, that's enough. There'll be no room for you!

Notice the way she *starts* the sentence with *and*, in this example. Children do this quite frequently as they approach age 3, often using it in places where you wouldn't really expect it to go. Here's Jamie at 2;10:

Mother: Where's the pushchair?
Jamie: And it's outside.

*"He said he wanted a clown for his birthday—at least that's
what I thought he said."*

And here's Eric (as early as 2;2) using it out of the blue. He puts a puppet in a box with other puppets and says:

> And I close them.

It's not clear whether children are using the word with meaning, in such cases, or whether they're just adding it on as a kind of habit. Either way, these sentences are odd.

But they don't last for long. As the third birthday approaches, you'll begin to hear these sentences used as part of a normal sequence. *And* starts joining two whole sentences together. This is the breakthrough.

Steven (2;11): Daddy gave me this, and it got broken.
Michael (3;0): That is like that on that side, and that is like that on that side.
Lucy (3;3): We wented to town, and we did have a haircut.

Why is this use of *and* a breakthrough? Because it's the first real sign of the use of 'complex sentences', as they're usually called in grammar books. All the examples of children's speech I have used so far have one thing in common. They're quite short. They contain just one Subject, Verb, Object, or whatever. Sentences like this:

> Me got a new car.   Where you going?
> Mummy's gone in the shop.

The grammars would call these 'simple sentences'.

In complex sentences, you get two of these shorter sentences being used at the same time – or more than two. They are joined together by a connecting word, or 'conjunction'. *And* is the first conjunction children learn.

The effect is striking. Immediately, children's utterances become twice as long as they were before. If you've been writing them down, you can use a ruler to prove it. One week they're saying 5- or 6-word sentences. The next week the sentences are a dozen words or more. Once children learn *and* in this way there's no stopping them. Soon a whole string of sentences come out, joined in the same way, limited only by the child's memory, shortage of

breath, or adult patience. Joanne (3;4) rushed in from the garden
one day, took a deep breath, and launched herself into this great
saga:

Daddy – daddy have breaked the spade all up and – and – and
it broken and – he did hurt his hand on it and – and – and – it's
gone all sore and . . .

We can stop Joanne there because the point of the example is
clear enough. However, there's something else to note about this
early complex sentence. The dashes represent pauses. Evidently,
the sentence is not coming out in a rush. It's being said in short
chunks which have a curious rhythm to them. If I put these
chunks one beneath the other, you'll see why it's curious:

Daddy have breaked the spade all up and/
and it broken and/
he did hurt his hand on it and/
it's gone all sore and/.

The *ands* are coming at the end of each chunk, instead of at the
beginning. If adults were to break this sentence up into chunks,
they would pause after the words *up*, *broken*, *it*, and *sore*. Children
often put the pauses in other places, as they try to cope with the
long utterance. The end-placed *and* is one of the commonest
patterns, though not all children do it as regularly as Joanne did.

There's another thing to note about this sentence. Joanne repeats *and* several times, and *daddy* is repeated also. This is another
very common feature of early complex sentences. It is as if children
need time to plan what they are going to say while they are
saying it. Joanne gets to the end of the first part of the utterance,
and then works out what to say next. The repeated use of *and*
shows her engine ticking over, as it were. The next part of the
utterance comes out in a rush, without pauses, and then she
slows down again. There is a slow-slow-quick-quick-slow rhythm
to a great deal of children's speech at this age.

About one in three children seem to have a great deal of trouble,
as they start to produce complex sentences. Their speech becomes
much jerkier, with pauses all over the place. They begin to repeat
not just single words but whole groups of words, as in this case:

I saw Mark and he gave me – he gave me – he gave me this
car.

Most noticeable of all, they start repeating single sounds, as
here:

The doggie ran across the road and he f- f-f- f- found hims
bone.

A stammer. Alarm bells! Panic stations! Dial 999. Which service
do you require? Speech therapy, quick.

No. As *The Hitch-hiker's Guide to the Galaxy* says on its cover:
Don't Panic. There's no need.

This kind of non-fluency is a perfectly normal development at
this age. Faced with the enormous task of making your sentences
twice as long, remembering twice as many things to say at once,
thinking ahead to what you want to say in the sentence after
next – it's enough to make *anyone* stammer! What's surprising is
that more children don't end up giving their parents a fright in
this way.

If it's left to itself, the stammer will last a few months, and then
die away. It may even affect simple sentences too – where it
sounds even more disturbing. One of my own children was a
textbook case. Ben stammered from 2;9 to 3;4, and then it gradually started to die away. If I hadn't known the facts, I'd have been
very worried. To be honest, I think I was worried anyway. Certainly, my wife and I both breathed a sigh of relief when it finally
stopped. Well, we're only human, and you can't always trust
these scientists . . .

What do I mean by saying 'leave it to itself'? Several things.
Don't get impatient with such children, as they try to get the
word out. Don't say things like 'Spit it out', 'Come on, I haven't
got all day', and the like. If you do that, you'll draw attention to
the stammer and you might make it worse. You have to realize
that the children themselves don't realize they're stammering.
You can tell that from the routine way in which they stand in
front of you, without a care in the world, producing a word's first
sounds perhaps a dozen times or more. They're not struggling to
get the sounds out, as an adult stammerer often does. There's no
sense of strain, or tension, or anxiety. The only people who
naturally feel anxious are the parents – and that's what you have

to try to hide. If you don't, the child will sense your anxiety, and that could lead to trouble. In fact, one of the main theories about why real stammering develops is based on this point. According to this theory, if children are harassed while working through this normal stage, they'll become nervous about their ability to say things fluently, and the stammer will stay.

Peggy Dalton, a speech therapist who specializes in stammering, once told me that parents should approach this normal non-fluency as they would a child who was learning to walk. You don't push children into walking or they'll continually fall over. You let them find their own feet. Every now and then you help them keep their balance. You take their hand to help them succeed. But you don't anxiously watch over their every step, in case they fall and hurt themselves. It's the same with stammering, she said. If a child seems to be getting cross because the word won't come, then by all means casually finish off the sentence, or suggest an alternative. Gentle guidance will do no harm.

Other complex sentences

Once children have overcome the *and* hurdle, they concentrate on developing their control of other kinds of complex sentence. Several new kinds of linking word appear. *And then* is one of the first, as they start to tell stories where lots of things happened. And then, during the fourth year, they begin to use *because* (often pronounced *'cos*), *so*, *if*, *what*, *when*, *but*, *or*, *that*, *where*, *while*, and several others. There's so much happening in such a short time that child language researchers usually talk about these conjunctions in groups, based on the meaning they express. Some of the most important groups are given below; the examples are all taken from children aged between 3 and 4½.

Time connections Many early complex sentences express the meaning of time. The child uses conjunctions like *and then* (or simply *and* or *then*), *when*, *while*, *before* and *after* to link the sentences.

> We went to the shops and then we went home.
> I let go when he pulls it hard.

I just get something from my room while Sesame Street
 gets to started.
Can I have a biscuit before I go to bed?

Cause connections Because, *so*, and *to* are the main conjunctions which express the meanings of cause and effect, result, or purpose (see p. 169). *And* can also be used in this way. (But *since* is a much later development. You won't hear that until well after age 5.)

I like it so much 'cos I haven't seen you wore it for a long time.
I know that, because she's in there.
Push it over there so he can sit on it.
You help us, daddy, so we can do it quicker more.
I must put my dress to go to the party on.
She got her sweetie and she's happy now.

Stating a contrast But is the main conjunction used for this meaning.

 I asked him, but he didn't want to come in.
 I was tired, but now I'm not tired.
 Our flip flops are like that, but one of them are brokened.
 It's the same as yesterday but 'cept it's a different biscuit.

It may even be used twice in a sentence – something that isn't usual in adult language:

But that one hasn't been grown, but that one has with the rain
 yesterday.

Stating an alternative   Or is the main conjunction.

 You sit there or I won't play any more.
 Put the cup on there or put it on there.

Expressing a condition The main conjunction is *if*, at this age. *Though*, *although*, *whether*, and *unless* also express conditions, but these aren't learned until much later.

 I don't know if you know that one.
 If I wear the other ones, they don't fall down.

Also at this age, children start making complex sentences which have question-words inside them, such as *what, who, why*, and *where*.

> I've got the clean socks what you asked me for.
> Tell me what it's called, mummy.
> I don't know why I got one like that.
> I know where to put it.
> I don't know who it is.

That is another common connecting word:

> I think that he will fall over.

But often the same kind of sentence is used with *that* omitted:

> This is the way I did it.
> Look at the toy I got.

or with *what* being used instead:

> Look at the toy what I got.

Some of these last types of sentence are in fact found very early in child speech, well before the age of 3.

By the middle of the fourth year, most children have started to say complex sentences which contain different kinds of connecting words. Needless to say, they often go badly wrong to begin with. A sentence starts out with one plan in mind, but the child loses track halfway through. This happened to Mark at age 3;9, when he bravely launched himself into a complicated thought. He gets to the end of the sentence all right, and there's no difficulty in understanding him, but his tense forms suffer badly in the process.

> If Father Christmas come down the chimney, and he will
> have presents when he came down, can I stay up to see
> him?

Lucy, at about the same age, tried the following sequence. She gets the tenses right, but the pronouns waver uncertainly.

> I had one, but it had a hole in it, didn't I.

A couple of months later, and she produced these:

When our pussy cats are good and they catch mouses we
   say good girls, don't we.
I'm not as big as you, but when I'm a mummy I'll be the
   same big.

It's remarkable progress to get to this stage within a year of
having no complex sentences at all. There's still a great deal to be
done, of course. Several of the more difficult conjunctions, such as
unless or *since*, have not yet been attempted, nor will they be until
age 8 or 9. And there are innumerable complications involved in
learning all the ways of attaching a sentence to a verb. English
makes you say *I want to eat a peach* and not *I want eating a peach*.
But with a verb like *see*, it's the other way round: *I saw her eating a*
peach and not *I saw her to eat a peach*. In addition, you can say *I*
saw her eat a peach. However, with *like*, you can say both *I like*
eating a peach as well as *I like to eat a peach* – but you can't say *I*
like eat a peach. Confused?

This is one of the most complicated areas of English grammar,
and it takes children several years to sort it all out. 'How did we
ever learn it all?', you might be thinking. With difficulty, is the
only answer. Here's Lucy again, getting into deep water over
what construction to use after *thank you*:

Thank you to wash my new dress what you made me.
Thank you for let me looking after him.

You'll hear many such errors in pre-school children and even the
best of them won't have mastered all the do's and don'ts until
around age 9.

Pronunciation

Between three and five, the child's language greatly increases in
quantity. Some of the most important rules of the language –
those to do with the order of words in a sentence, for instance –
have been largely mastered; and they have a working vocabulary
which must be approaching 5,000 words. Fortunately, their
pronunciation has been keeping pace with these developments.
By about $3\frac{1}{2}$ all the vowels should be in use, as should most of
the consonants. In David Olmsted's study of pronunciation of

children at age 4, there were only a few consonants which still posed problems:

- [l] in the middle and at the end of a word, as in *yellow* and *full*;
- the *ng* sound in words like *sing* and *singer*;
- [t] in the middle of a word;
- the two *th* sounds, as in *this* and *thin*;
- [z] at the beginning of a word;
- the consonant sound heard in words like *judge*;
- the consonant sound heard in the middle of words like *pleasure*;
- the *ch* sound in the middle of a word (as in *teacher*).

By 5, only some of the more subtle friction consonants cause any problems. Children at this age may still be having difficulty distinguishing such pairs of words as *fin* and *thin*, for example, or *sin* and *shin*, and these difficulties may show up in the way they pronounce these words. [w] and [r] may still be confused, as when *red* comes out as [wed]. But on the whole, pronunciation errors with single consonants are found only in long or unfamiliar words. When children hear a word such as *disturb*, for instance, they often pronounce the final *b* as [v] – though they would never normally mix up [b] and [v] in this way.

There is, however, one very important development in pronunciation which takes place mainly in the pre-school period, and that is the joining of consonants together to produce acceptable versions of such words as *spin*, *break*, *jump*, and *box* (which has *two* sounds at the end, [ks], even though there's only one letter). These 'consonant clusters' first make their appearance in the middle or at the end of words during the third year; but children take two or more years to master them.

You have to appreciate the size of the problem. There are 22 single consonants in most English accents, but there are over 300 ways of joining them together. These include such 'doubles' as [pl-], [pr-], [sl-], and [kr-], and such 'triples' as [spl-] and [str-]. There are even some 'quadruples' but these only occur at the end of words, as in *glimpsed* [glimpst], and are not very frequent. A list of the commonest consonant clusters is given in Appendix 3 (p. 230), with space to tick them off as you hear them emerge in your own child.

Why does it take so long? One reason is that there are big differences between the clusters which can be used at the beginning of a word in English, and those which can be used at the end. A cluster like [tr-] can be used at the beginning, as in *tray*; but there are no words ending in *-tr* in English. Likewise, [-mp] can only be used at the end of a word, as in *jump*; there are no words starting with *mp-* in English. Nearly all of the 'double' clusters are like this. [st] and a few others can be used in both places, as in *stop* and *must*.

David Allerton studied one child's learning of the 'double' clusters at the beginning of words between the ages of 3;9 and 5;3. At age 4, this child was able to pronounce 14 consonants at the beginning of words, but he had no clusters at all. The first signs of a cluster began to emerge at around 4;3, with the use of [sl]. He used this to pronounce adult words beginning with *sl-*, and also for words beginning with *pl-*, *kl-*, and *fl-*. He must have noticed that [sl] doesn't have any vibration of the vocal cords (there's no 'buzzing' noise while you say these sounds – unlike [bl] or [gl]) – and so he used the same sequence for other clusters which also lack this vibration.

By 4;9 he had learned [sm] as in *smile*, and was using [bw] for a whole range of adult clusters – *br-*, *dr-*, *dw-*, *gr-*, *bl-* and *gl-*. Six months later and there was far more happening. He was still using [sm] and [sl] correctly and by this time he was using [pl], [fl] and [sn] correctly too. But when he tried to pronounce the others, he would get them wrong. Adult *gl-* came out as [dl]; *kr-* and *kw-* came out as [kf]; *kl-* came out as [tl]; and *pr-* came out as [pf]. It's interesting that several of these pronunciations are used in foreign languages – [pf], for instance, is heard in such German words as *pfennig* – but they aren't used in English.

By 5½, there was a sudden leap in ability: he became able to produce almost any cluster as long as he spoke slowly. Allerton puts this down to the fact that in school during this period the child was learning to 'sound words out', using a phonic approach. But 5½ is really quite a late age to master these pronunciations. Many children are anything up to a year ahead of this, learning almost all their clusters (including many 'triples') before they go to school.

Dealing with errors

Children pay the penalty of success during their fourth and fifth years. Partly as a result of the progress they have made in pronunciation, grammar and vocabulary, their errors tend to stand out more. Because they're doing so much right, it becomes even more noticeable when they do something wrong. There's no justice!

It's a time when parents often get very finicky about their children's language and frequently correct errors in grammar and pronunciation. At earlier ages this hardly ever happens, except in very indirect ways. Parents of 2-year-olds are likely to correct a wrong word – *that's not a dog, that's a cat*, they might say – but they don't usually draw their child's attention to an immature pronunciation or erroneous grammatical usage. I've never heard a conversation like the following:

Child (2;0): Daddy gone.
Mother: No, listen, darling. Daddy's gone.

Some parents may be like that, but most aren't. As we've seen (p. 114), most respond positively to what their children are trying to say at this age. They accept the meaning of what is said, and give only an indirect clue that there may be better ways of saying it.

Child: Daddy gone.
Mother: That's right, darling. Daddy's gone, hasn't he?

But by 3½ or so things have changed, and dialogues in which parents hammer away at sound and grammar are much more common. One of the most famous examples in the history of child language studies is of this kind. It was observed by David McNeill in the early 1960s.

Child: Nobody don't like me.
Mother: No, say 'Nobody likes me'.
Child: Nobody don't like me.
Mother: No, say 'Nobody likes me'.

Child: Nobody don't like me.
(*This exchange is repeated seven more times, and then*)
Mother: No, now listen carefully. Say 'Nobody likes me'.
Child: Oh! Nobody don't likes me.

There's a two-fold irony in this exchange. The mother was concerned about the double negative *Nobody don't*, but when the child finally decides to alter his speech, he simply adds the *-s* ending to the verb, and leaves the double negative alone. The other irony, of course, as has often been pointed out, is how a mother can focus on a point of grammar when the child is saying something as heart-rending as 'Nobody likes me'!

There's a big linguistic lesson to be learned here. This dialogue shows that children cannot be made to run linguistically before they can walk. This child seems to be at a certain stage in the development of his language, a stage at which he uses two negative words in the same sentence. It is in fact a perfectly normal stage of development in learning how to say no (as we've seen, p. 134). And he can't be rushed out of it and on to the next stage. He even finds it difficult to imitate what his mother has just said. And even if he *had* managed to imitate the sentence to please his mother, it's unlikely that he would have been able to carry on using it in his everyday speech afterwards. Six months later, though, and he would be saying 'Nobody likes me' as well as any of us do!

The same principle applies to pronunciation. A child who can't manage an [r] sound, and who says [wed] for *red* or [bwik] for *brick* is doing a perfectly normal thing. In fact, it's so normal that to call it an 'error' is really quite misleading. Children are unable to do anything about it, until their ability to make certain distinctions with their lips and tongue reaches a particular stage. They then slip into making the distinction quite naturally. They won't be rushed. And parents who don't like a particular pronunciation, at this age, won't get anywhere if they try to change it. Everyone will get upset, and that's all.

Parents have rather more success in the field of 'social' language teaching, during the fourth year. They introduce their children to such words as *please* and *thank you* (or one of its forms, such as *ta*). They draw attention to various rules of politeness, such as the use of *Mr* before a name, or the need to control the voice (*Don't shout, it's rude*). Children seem very able to pick up social rules of this kind. In fact, parents are often quite embarrassed at how accurately their children learn these rules, when they hear them playing with their toys. One mother turned bright red at a coffee morning when her 4-year-old was heard to say to her doll: 'Now Jenny, you say please or you'll get a big spank on your bot!'

The fourth and fifth years of life provide us with innumerable examples of linguistic errors as children try to sort out the rules of the language around them. Most of the errors are in the field of grammar, because this is the area in which the most complicated kinds of learning are taking place. We've already seen some of the difficulties posed by the pronouns, irregular nouns and verbs, questions, and other kinds of construction. Children have made considerable progress in all these areas by age 4, but there is so much to get through. Even at 9 or 10, occasional errors can still be made. Susie (see Chapter 1) had mastered all irregular verbs except one at age 11. She would still sometimes say *tooken* instead of *taken*, especially when she was tired or irritable. Come to think of it, the other day I heard myself saying *brung* instead of *bring*. Will it ever end?

There's no space to illustrate all the kinds of error which can be heard in the fifth year. Here's a small selection.

1. Mixing up two constructions:

I'm going to make a different picture – quite a very difficult one.
Four green sweets, how old as me!
Is that one your favourite best?
I can reach a little bit of that high.

Father: Stand a bit nearer.
Child: It's all the nearer I can stand.

2. Problems with prepositions:

I made him happy of by doing good to him.
You're being helpful of this game.
I'll be home at late.
I'm bored at shopping.

3. Words in the wrong order:

We have each six.
I must put my dress to go to the party on.
I've got lots of Katys my friends (= 'lots of friends called
   Katy').
Are we going on the bus home?

4. Time words muddled:

At playgroup today the other week . . .
This morning tomorrow you can come to my house.

5. Unclear pronouns:

A little girl fell over in playgroup and hurt herself on a chair
   and it was bleeding.
One day a boy went for a walk in the woods, and he saw her
   by the lake.

6. Problems with verbs:

You know what daddy letted to Ben? He letted him keep a
   paper.
He shouldn't have lost it, could he?

7. Problems with *any*:

He hasn't got any much hair, has he?
There wasn't any else.

8. Problems with *much*:

He hasn't got very much toys.
Are there much cakes for tea?

Faced with such boundless inventiveness, what is a parent to
do? Explicit correction is unlikely to have much of an effect. On
the other hand, a policy of ignoring every error isn't very satis-
factory either. It's only natural to want to help, to point out
errors, in language as in any other walk of life. And in a few
months' time, the children are going to enter an environment in
which explicit correction is the rule. Maybe they'd better get some
practice in being corrected, before the schoolteachers get their
hands on them?

I think a balanced diet of ignoring, gentle ear-jogging, asking questions and firmly correcting is the only solution. I would ignore an error if it turned up while the child was in full flow, telling you all about something which happened. It wouldn't be right to interrupt, stop the story, correct the grammar, and then invite the child to carry on.

By 'gentle ear-jogging', I mean giving the correct version of a sentence, if an opportunity arises, just after the child's version. It's the same approach as is used when parents of younger children expand their speech (see p. 114). *He shouldn't have lost it, could he*, says the child. *No, he shouldn't, should he*, replies the parent, gently but clearly.

Questions can be very helpful. The vast majority of the errors above don't interfere with the meaning. It's clear enough what the child meant to say. But occasionally it won't be clear, and in these circumstances you have to ask a question to sort out the ambiguity. Of course, you may well get your come-uppance:

Child: You can put as much sugar on.
Mother: As much as what?
Child: As much as you like.

Last, the occasional explicit correction will do no harm as long as it's done in a kindly manner. A single correction will do:

Child: I got too much cars.
Mother: Too *many* cars, darling.

Don't be persistent, and ask the child to repeat the correct form back. This won't work. But *do* be consistent. If you decide that *much* is your *bête noire*, then try to provide a reasonable supply of correct forms whenever you notice the error. Otherwise what is the child to think? 'Sometimes they correct me; sometimes they don't. There must be an even more subtle grammatical rule here than I ever dreamed of!'

To conclude

I mustn't leave you here with the impression that the pre-school child produces nothing but errors. On the contrary. You can listen to sentence after sentence and hear nothing wrong at all. That's what I'd expect, most of the time – fluent, confident, error-free speech. The errors come only when the child is breaking fresh ground, trying out new constructions. That's why they're so important. They're the main evidence we have of the exact point that a child's language learning has reached. But for most of everyday conversation, children use the same kinds of sentences they've used before, in the same kinds of ways, and they don't have any errors in them.

I first found this out when I once transcribed the conversation of two 4½-year-olds and went through the transcript with my blue pencil at the ready, looking for errors. I found about a dozen in twenty pages. Some pages had no blue marks on at all. Later, I was discussing this point with a teacher, who said, 'Well, that's it, then. If they're not making mistakes any more, they must have finished learning the grammar of their language. Language acquisition's over. There's nothing more to be acquired.' A plausible view. But he was wrong, as you'll see in the next chapter.

Feature 15 | Passive learning

There are many sentences in English which can turn up in either of two forms. *Active* sentences are those like *The man saw the cat* or *The girl kicked the ball*. *Passive* sentences are those like *The cat was seen by the man* or *The ball was kicked by the girl* – or simply, *The cat was seen* or *The ball was kicked*. Passive sentences are much less common in everyday speech. The difference between the two is often no more than a difference of emphasis, but sometimes there's more to it. No 9-year-old – or 19-year-old – is likely to say, straight off, *I just broke the window*, using an active sentence. They'll probably prefer the passive, using a sentence like *The window's just been broken*, which hints that it might have been someone else's fault, maybe even the window's!

Brian Baldie published a report in 1976 of the way children learned this distinction. He studied 100 children between 3 and 8. The experimenter gave each child a set of cards on which different situations were drawn. For example, one set showed the following five situations:

a boy chasing a girl
a girl chasing a boy
a girl and a boy running side by side
a boy and a girl running in opposite directions
a boy and a girl running towards each other.

The experimenter then said a sentence out loud, such as *The boy was chased by the girl*, and the children had to point to the correct picture.

This part of the study showed how far the children could *understand* passive sentences. Baldie also did two other things. He got the children to *imitate* a passive sentence. The experimenter would say a passive sentence to the child and the child had to say it back straight away. And he also tried to get the children to *say* passive sentences spontaneously, by asking them questions about the pictures. 'What has happened to the girl?' he would ask, hoping that the children would say 'The girl's been chased by the boy', or some similar sentence.

The results were very interesting. Baldie found that there was a steady growth in the children's ability to handle the passive construction over the whole period. It took them *five years* to learn, and even at 8, only 80 per cent of the children were able to produce passive sentences along the above lines. Here are some details.

– Ten children were tested at age 3–3½. None of them was able to produce any passives. But the group scored 17 out of 30 correct in the comprehension part of the experiment, and there was a similar score for the imitation part.

– A year later, and the children were imitating the passive sentences correctly all the time. They got a score of 26 out of 30 for comprehension. And they were beginning to produce some passives as well – 4 out of 30.

– There was very little difference between ages 5 and 6. But from the seventh year, there was a marked increase in their ability to produce passives. The 6-year-old group produced 14 out of 30. This group also obtained a score of 26 out of 30 for comprehension. And perfect scores for imitation, of course.

– By age 8, imitation was perfect and comprehension nearly so (29 out of 30). However, production was still only 16 out of 30. Twenty per cent of the subjects at this age produced no passives at all.

It's quite clear from this that complete mastery of the passive is by no means achieved for all children by 8. They've all learned to imitate these sentences before 5. They're pretty well perfect in comprehension by about 7. But they don't even begin to produce passives on average until well into their fourth year, and other studies suggest that they're still sorting this aspect out after they're 9!

Why should it take so long? One reason is that there are several different kinds of passive sentence, and some are more difficult than others. It's been found, for instance, that passive sentences which contain an 'action' verb (like *push* or *kick*) are learned more quickly than those which contain a verb of 'experiencing' (such as *see* or *like*). And the type of construction can make a difference too. Baldie looked at three kinds of passive.

– One type can be used 'both ways round'. *The boy was chased by the girl* can 'reverse' into *The girl was chased by the boy*.

– The second type can't reverse. *The house was painted by the man* can't change into *The man was painted by the house*.

– In the third type, it isn't clear who did the action. *The nail was bent*.

In Baldie's study, the children seemed to have greater difficulty with the first type, especially in the early period of learning; and other studies have found the same thing. When young children hear a sentence like *The boy was chased by the girl* they tend to interpret it as if it were 'The boy was chasing the girl'.

You can prove this for yourself, if you happen to have access to a tame 4- or 5-year-old. Give the child a male and a female doll. Check they can tell that one is a boy and one is a girl. Then say: 'Show me *The boy is chasing the girl*'. The child will pick up the boy doll and make it run after the girl. Next, do something else for a while, to take the child's mind off the task. Then say: 'Show me *The boy is chased by the girl*'. Five-year-olds will probably make the boy chase the girl *again* – as if they had heard only 'Boy – chase – girl'. Seven-year-olds will on the whole carry out the task correctly, and make the girl chase the boy.

I did this experiment once and thought I'd better check that the children had heard the crucial word *by*: so I said it very loud, *The boy is chased BY the girl*. It didn't make any difference to the 5-year-olds except that one tiny scrap looked me straight in the eye, looked down at the dolls, carefully placed the two dolls side by side, and made them both chase together away into the distance. They were both chasing BY (= 'next to') each other. I went home and had a long gin and tonic.

Feature 16 | Does after come before or does before come after?

One of the problems children have to sort out when they're learning complex sentences is which way round things go. Take these four cases:

1. Mary laughed, as the clock struck three.
2. As the clock struck three, Mary laughed.
3. The clock struck three, as Mary laughed.
4. As Mary laughed, the clock struck three.

What is the child to make of this? Do these sentences mean the same thing, or not? You and I know that, apart from slight differences in emphasis, there's no change in meaning. Children should be able to work this out for themselves in a fairly short time.

In fact, sentences like these aren't all learned at the same time, during the pre-school years. Children seem to find 1 easier than 2, and 3 easier than 4, and thus come out with 1 and 3 earlier. Why is this? Basically because children like to have the main point in a sentence said first. In 1 and 2, 'Mary laughing' is the main point (the 'main clause' in the sentence, grammar books would say). In 3 and 4, 'The clock striking' is the main point. Putting first the less important point (the 'subordinate clause', which always begins with the connecting word) is something they prefer to do later.

These sentences don't present much of a problem because the meaning is the same each time. However, other connecting words which express time are much more difficult to sort out – *before* and *after*, in particular. Let's begin with *before*, which is fairly straightforward.

> Mary laughed, before the clock struck three.
> Before the clock struck three, Mary laughed.

So far, so good. You'd expect children to learn the first before the second, on the above principle.

Now let's turn to *after*.

Mary laughed, after the clock struck three.
After the clock struck three, Mary laughed.

Here a complication sets in. You'd expect children to have no trouble with the first of these, because 'Mary laughing' comes first, and that's the main clause. But they *do* have trouble.

You can try this experiment on pre-school children, to show that there's a problem. What they have to do is carry out your instructions in the order you say. Start with an easy sequence.

'Touch your nose and then touch your tummy.'

Do a few of these, so that the child gets the idea. Then switch to *after*.

'Touch your nose after you touch your tummy.'

You'll find that the children will still touch their nose *first*, even though your sentence asked them to touch their tummy first.

That's the trouble with *after*, when it comes in the second part of the sentence. It's the second thing that's said but the first thing that happens. It's a back-to-front way of saying things. And, not surprisingly, children don't much like it. They assume that the first thing that's said happens first; the second thing that's said happens second. They follow the order in which you mention things.

Now look at this sentence the other way round:

'After you touch your tummy, touch your nose.'

This is much easier for children to cope with. The order of the clauses corresponds to the order of events, so that's all right. However, you'll notice that the main clause doesn't come first, so some children will still find this slightly complicated.

That's not all. Let's go back to *before*. *Before* raises a similar problem, but in reverse. (I hope you're following all this! But if *you're* having difficulty, you can imagine the child's problems.) Compare these two sentences:

'Touch your nose, before you touch your tummy.'
'Before you touch your tummy, touch your nose.'

The first sentence should cause no difficulty. The main clause comes first, and the sequence of events expressed by the language follows the sequence of events which should take place.

But the second sentence is really awkward. The main clause comes second, *and* the order of events is the wrong way round. Children will have trouble with that one too.

It really is a minefield. And several other factors influence the way in which children learn to cope with these differences. For instance, if the relationship between the two parts of the sentence is logical, they find the sentence easier than if it isn't. Compare these two sentences:

John put his raincoat on before he went out.
John put his raincoat on before the television set broke down.

Children find it much easier to use *before/after* sentences when they can see a reason for joining the sentences together.

Most children seem to find *before* sentences easier than *after* sentences. So it's possible to summarize all this by saying that these children find the following increase in difficulty, for the four types of sentence we've been talking about:

easiest is 'X happened before Y happened'
next is 'After X happened, Y happened'
next is 'Before X happened, Y happened'
and the most difficult is 'X happened after Y happened'.

There seem to be several exceptions, though. Some children use *after* before *before* – or *before* after *after*, if you prefer.

If you feel like another drink at this point, I sympathize. But we're not just playing games with language. If we know that children have these difficulties with language, then we can try to make things easier for them, when it's really important. In school, for instance, they'll meet sentences like these:

Before you do question 3, revise the topic you did on page 1.

I wonder how many children have found question 3 harder than they expected, because they read the first part of the sentence, and got on with it immediately? It would be so much easier if the instruction were:

Revise the topic you did on page 1, before you do question 3.

Likewise, how many children have been told off for not paying attention, when they hear:

Now, before you go out to play, I want you to put all your things away! . . . Johnny Smith, I said put your things away first!

No, teacher, you didn't.

Feature 17 | If only . . .

When do children learn to use *if*? The general view is: quite late. Several studies have suggested that *if*-sentences don't turn up much before 6 or 7 years of age. If they do, children are likely to get them wrong. They say things like:

> If they put him in between, he wants to go there.

Nor do they find *if*-sentences easy to understand. If you present young children with two sentences, one logical and one illogical, they don't seem able to tell the difference. They'll be happy to accept both the following, for instance:

> I wear a coat if the weather is cold. (*Logical.*)
> The lake is frozen if I want to go skating. (*Illogical.*)

In a study by Harriet Emerson in 1980, children didn't begin to tell these apart until age 7. The concept of 'conditional meaning', which *if* expresses, seems to be quite a difficult one to grasp.

However, a survey of children's spontaneous speech carried out by a Canadian team of child language researchers, led by Ann McCabe, led to a different conclusion. There were 48 children in the study, divided into 24 pairs of siblings. Each sibling-pair was recorded for an hour, without adults present. The children ranged in age from 2;10 to 7;3.

If turned out not to be very common: only 82 *if*-sentences were found in all of the samples. But it was used much more frequently than the researchers had expected. Even the youngest child (of 2;10) was found to produce such a sentence, and nearly 40 per cent of the 3-year-olds did. Altogether, over 60 per cent of the children produced at least one *if*-sentence. None of the sentences contained the kind of logical error noted above, though a few contained grammatical errors, such as:

> If you were a paint monster, then it will. (Answering the question 'Does paint taste nice?')

Why should these children be producing so many *if*-sentences? The answer lies in the way they were using these sentences. Here are some of the meanings that were expressed:

Cause and effect – If you drink paint, you'll get sick.

Expressing a consequence – I have to make a line for us, if you want to play.

Sharing a belief – You can't go to sleep, can you, if it's daytime.

Making a general correlation – I want the ball, if it fits.

Bribes and threats – I'll put it back if you give me that fence.

Expressing personal intention – Jamie, if you're thirsty, know what I would do?

Expressing a physical relationship – What's it going to be if it dries up?

Expressing a social relationship – You know, if you're finished with that, you should put it away.

Expressing a potential relationship – If you curl, you're dead.

Nearly 40 per cent of the *if*-sentences used by the children to each other were 'bribes and threats'. For some of them, this was the *only* kind of conditional sentence they used. That goes a long way towards explaining why adults don't hear children use many such sentences. Children don't usually threaten or bribe the adults they're talking to!

But there's a more general implication. In the McCabe study, the children were playing together, in a familiar setting, with familiar toys. There was no pressure, and they could talk about whatever they wanted. This is a very different world from that of the linguistic experiment, where researchers ask children strange questions about unfamiliar objects. Perhaps, then, the main reason why people have underestimated children's ability to use *if* is that they have been looking for it in the wrong place.

Feature 18 | Just because

The man's fallen off the ladder because he's broken his leg.

You've probably heard children say something like this from around the fourth year. Or you may have seen the same kind of error turning up when they get to school, and begin to write simple stories. Why do they do it?

When child language researchers first studied this topic, they found lots of back-to-front sentences as young children tried to express cause and effect. They concluded that such errors are caused by children being unable to perceive cause-and-effect relationships in the outside world until they're quite old. The correct use of *because*, they argued, won't be present until 7 or 8 years, when their ability to reason is so much more developed. Before then, the children are confused, so there'll be lots of back-to-front sentences.

This can't be the total explanation. It might work for some of the less obvious chains of cause and effect which children meet up with – such as *It's raining because the flowers are growing* – but it will hardly work for those areas of experience which children know something about. The child who said the sentence about falling off a ladder was nearly 5. He knew very well that if you fall down you get hurt. But he still said the sentence the other way round.

A rather more likely reason is that children didn't do so well because they found the experimenters' tasks unfamiliar. Most of the sentences which are usually used to test children's understanding are like the one at the top of the page. The two events are quite separate: falling off the ladder ends before breaking the leg begins. But in everyday speech, *because* links events which are not so clearly distinct. They may overlap, or even be simultaneous. Consider such sentences as:

> She went there because she wanted to.
> I like reading because it's fun.

The reading doesn't stop before the fun begins. Both 'events' take place at the same time.

In a 1984 study by Allyssa McCabe and Carole Peterson, it was found that over two-thirds of the *because*-sentences children use were like these last two. And children were using *because* far more often than anyone expected. Moreover, far fewer mistakes were being made in its use. The crucial difference is that McCabe and Peterson were studying the use of this word in the children's spontaneous speech, and not in an artificial experiment.

Ninety-six children aged between $3\frac{1}{2}$ and $9\frac{1}{2}$ were asked to tell stories about themselves. Altogether, 1,124 stories were told. The word *because* was found to turn up 437 times, and *so* (another important cause-and-effect word) 495 times. Both words were very popular, even at the younger ages.

They found that 60 per cent of the children's *because* sentences expressed the meaning of causality quite correctly, and only 7 were in the wrong order. Similarly, 38 per cent of the *so* sentences referred to causality, with only 1 being in the wrong order. Even the 4-year-olds did quite well.

Two out of three uses of *because* and eight out of nine uses of *so* were correct, even at the youngest ages. The children said such things as:

She wanted to hurt him, so she hit him.
I scratched her, so she scratched me.
My dad didn't get to go because he had to work.
I couldn't swim, so I walked in the water.
You shouldn't throw rocks, because that will break windows.
He painted it grey because I don't know why he wanted to.
There was one Easter egg missing because I hided it and
couldn't remember where I hided it at.

What were the *because* errors like? McCabe and Peterson classify them into nine types:

1. The child fails to explain the causal link straight away (but it is explained eventually).

My mom and dad think I got an allergy because we have
leaves in back of the house. And I came out. I was there about
ten minutes and I came right back, and my eyes were
watering . . .

2. The child fails to explain the causal link, and never gets round to it.
My sister broke her arm when she fell off a minibike. She went to the doctor, so my Dad gave me a spanking.

3. The two events are linked by some fairly obvious third factor, which isn't explained.
She has to get five shots (= 'injections'), because she's in a wheelchair.

4. There is no obvious connection between the two parts of the sentence.
I was there with my other cousin because I couldn't stay with my little doll.

5. One event sets the stage for another, but doesn't directly cause it.
Every time I wanted something he'd pinch me, because he has those long fingernails.

6. One event follows the other in time, but does not cause it.
I fell and hurted my neck, because I had to go to the doctor's to get the shot for my mumps.

7. The second part of the sentence explains how someone knew what happened in the first part.
He got in a wreck and he died right in the place where he was, because Dad came by and saw it.

8. The second part of the sentence repeats the message of the first part, but in different words.
We already had one dog left, because we had Brownie.

9. The two parts repeat each other exactly.
I'm hungry because I'm hungry.

Both correct and incorrect uses of *because* were found throughout the whole age range. Children of nine may be a lot more aware of cause-and-effect than children at four, but 4-year-olds still have a lot they can tell us about the world, if we only listen.

If you're interested in a particular feature of a child's language development, you can discover quite a lot of information about it by simply asking them to imitate you. All you do is ask the child to 'Say what I say'. You say the sentence containing the feature which interests you, and the child repeats it back.

Why is imitation interesting? The point is that children will perform at their own linguistic level. If they repeat your sentence back to you perfectly, it doesn't prove very much. They might just have a very good memory and be good at parroting. But if they change your sentence in some way, this can give you a good indication of which bits of the sentence they find difficult, or aren't able to handle.

Here are some cases where the imitation was interesting:

Adult: Say 'I can see three more mice'.
Child (2;6): I see three mouses.

Adult: Say 'The cat was chased by the dog'.
Child (5;0): The cat is chasing a dog.

Adult: Say 'Where has daddy gone?'
Child (2;3): Where daddy gone?

Well, I say 'simply' . . .! Nothing is ever simple in child language studies. Here are a couple of cases when things didn't go according to plan:

Adult: Say 'I've got a hat on'.
Child: No, you haven't!

Adult: Now I want you to say exactly what I say, all right?
Lucy (3;0): Yes.
Adult: Are you sure, now?
Lucy: (*nods*)

Adult: All right, then, listen carefully. 'The man's running.'
Lucy: (*silence*)
Adult: Shall I say it again?
Lucy: (*nods*)
Adult: 'The man's running'. Now you say it.
Lucy: Want to go wee-wee.

One of the easiest ways of showing progress in a child's language is to put a set of sentences together, of different levels of difficulty, and ask the child to say them after you every few months. You'll notice the difference, as more of the sentences come to be repeated accurately. Start off with some very short and simple utterances, such as *Hello, Running,* and *Green*; then move on to longer ones, such as *Man running* or *Kick a ball*; and so on. A typical set of sentences is given in Appendix 4 (p. 232), along with a space to mark whether your child got them right, nearly right, or totally wrong.

However, if you do this sort of thing, there are a few points to remember.

1. Don't get so involved with the exercise that it ceases to be fun, for all concerned. If the child doesn't want to play, then don't play. If you start off, and the child gets bored or upset after a while, then stop immediately.

2. This isn't a test. You shouldn't be thinking 'How well will my child do?' The aim is simply to show up some of the areas of language which your child is currently grappling with.

3. Similarly, if the child stumbles at a sentence, don't go back over it until the sentence comes out right. I say again, this isn't a test. It's the stumble that you're supposed to be interested in.

4. You can make up other sentences on the same pattern, if you find the ones in the Appendix unclear or off-putting in some way. It won't make any difference if the sentences talk about cats, dogs, cows or pigs. If words in my list are difficult for the child (for instance, difficult to pronounce), change them.

5. You don't have to complete the whole exercise if the child grinds to a halt in the middle. Young children simply won't be able to cope with the longer sentences, and they'll lapse into silence, or ask to do something else. That's fine. Let them. Put the page away until another day.

6. Nor do you have to do the whole exercise all at once. If the child doesn't concentrate on things for very long, you may have to split it up anyway. Do a few sentences here and a few there – whenever everyone's in the mood.

7. However, each time you decide to carry out the exercise, start at the top – even though you know the child can do the short sentences. It's as well to start children off with a few sentences they can do, before plying them with the more difficult ones.

8. Leave a good gap between the occasions when you carry out the exercise – at least three months, I'd say, otherwise you might not see any change.

9. Give the child plenty of time to reply, after you say each sentence. If there's no immediate reply, say it a second time. Then move on. If you get total silence after three successive sentences, give up.

10. If you're not tape recording, be on your toes to note down the child's response as soon as it happens. In Appendix 4, there are lines drawn against each sentence. I suggest you place a tick on the left of the line if the child's imitation is perfectly correct (ignoring any differences in pronunciation or emphasis). Put the tick on the right of the line if the child makes a complete hash of it. And put the tick in the middle if there are just one or two small inaccuracies.

11. Lastly, a word of warning. Just because children can imitate something doesn't mean that they'll be able to say it in their spontaneous speech. A child might imitate *mice* one moment, and then be saying *mouses* the next. Nor should you expect the children to be able to understand everything they imitate. Even grown-up children sometimes copy what other people say without understanding it!

My son, aged about 4, started to use the expletive 'Christ!' rather too frequently. I didn't want to give him the idea that this was something bad, in case it made him say it all the more, so I asked him what he thought this word meant. He explained, 'It means there's no room in the car-park.'

Angela (7;0): I was at church on Sunday.
Friend (10;0): I didn't know you went to church. Are you a Catholic or a Protestant?
Angela: Neither. I'm a Brownie.

My son, aged 4, was a keen observer of his 9-year-old chess-playing brother. One day, I arrived back from church and told the family, 'The Bishop was there this morning.' He asked: 'Were the pawns there too?'

Lawrence (5;0) (*pointing a toy gun at his mother*): Fridge!

We were out visiting friends, during which an informal cup of tea was offered, accompanied by cake. We were sitting in easy chairs around the room, not at the table. My son, aged 3½, was offered a piece of cake, which he took. There was silence.

Mother: What do you say, dear?
Son (*disapprovingly*): No plate!

Heather, at age 2, had brought her interlocking bricks into her mother's bed and was busy building something when she discovered that the final brick was missing.

Heather: Where's the brick, mummy?
Mother: Here it is.
Heather: Thank you, mummy.
Mother (*solemnly*): It's a pleasure.
Heather: No. A chimney.

Vicar: We will say together the words which Jesus taught us.
Monica (3;0) (*loud whisper*): You didn't tell me Jesus had a
   tortoise, mummy.

Mary (5;0) (*just returned from Sunday school*): What does
   'art' mean?
Mother: Art is painting.
Mary: Well, next Sunday I shall say 'Our Father which is
   painting in heaven'. It sounds much nicer.

Vicky (4;0) was standing obediently by her father's elbow, as he
wrote busily at his desk in the study. Her eyes strayed across to
the three letter-trays stacked in order: 'In – Pending – Out'.

Vicky: Daddy, what does 'pending' mean?
Father: Waiting for attention.
Vicky: I'm pending, aren't I?

Shirley (5;0) (*looking at things for a jumble sale*): What's in
   that bottle?
Teacher: Toilet water, dear.
Shirley: Toilet water? But what's it for?
Teacher: To make you smell nice.
Shirley (*no reply, but the face said it all*)

Comment

These are all examples which show children making up their own
minds about the meaning of the words they hear around them,
and the contexts in which they should (or shouldn't) be used.
Most of the errors are quite unexpected – but as soon as they're
made, we can see the logic behind them. A linguistic commentary
is quite unnecessary.

6 | The Early School Years

'For this relief, much thanks!' said a taut father once, as total silence descended at a 5-year-old's birthday party, during a game of 'Dead Lions'. But it didn't last long. The language was back, with a vengeance, within minutes. How many shattered parents look back on the three hours or so of non-stop, excited vocalization and wonder whether language acquisition is an invention of the devil? At the very least, survivors of such parties must be wondering why this book has a Chapter 6 at all.

For most 5-year-olds are very fluent beings. To hear them at play must surely convey the impression that the period of language acquisition has come to an end. They say so much and they understand so much. There's nothing more to learn. That must be it. Language acquired. Allgone.

This view has in fact often been put forward in books on child development – especially some which have been written with teachers in mind. The argument goes like this. The speed of language acquisition is fantastic. You only have to listen to 5-year-olds to hear that. It therefore follows that children have completed the learning of their language before they get to school. There's nothing more for parent and teacher to do, apart from giving them the opportunity to use language in a wider and more demanding range of situations. There's certainly no need to do any formal language teaching.

It's a tempting view and if it were correct this book would indeed stop here. But it isn't correct. Language acquisition isn't finished by age 5. We've already seen this in earlier chapters, when we looked at the way in which children get to grips with some of the more complex grammatical constructions. They start learning auxiliary verbs, passives, *because*, pronouns, and many other features at various ages between 1 and 5, and they make considerable progress. But repeatedly we've seen that the learning

"Have you got a book about a little girl who lives in a lovely house and one day a fairy gives her three wishes and all lovely flowers come up all over the garden and she meets a unicorn and she finds a magic box and her Mummy comes and calls her in for tea?"

Children's Library, Quentin Blake

isn't over by the time they go to school. There are still many errors to be sorted out. And there are thus many ways in which teacher and parent can help.

New structures to learn

The easiest way to see that the learning of grammar isn't over is to do a kind of subtraction sum. Adult grammar minus 5-year-old grammar = ? I don't know what the figure is, but the answer is undoubtedly 'a lot'. There are many constructions which adults use routinely that are well beyond the abilities of a 5-year-old. This piece of dialogue illustrates one common feature.

Mary: See you at 5.
John: Where?
Mary: Outside Woolworth's.
(*The next day.*)
Mary: Where were you? I waited for ages, but you didn't show up.
John: What do you mean? I was waiting for *you*!
Mary: Well, you weren't outside Woolworth's, like we agreed.
John: Woolworth's? It was outside Marks you said we'd meet, wasn't it?

Let me spell out that last sentence:
It was outside Marks
(that) you said
(that) we'd meet
wasn't it?

Four different kinds of clauses attached to each other, the whole thing being said very quickly and fluently. No 5-year-old ever came out with a sentence like this. I wouldn't expect to find such constructions used until a child was 8 or 9.

But the most noticeable difference between 5-year-old speech and adult speech is the way in which strings of sentences come to be joined together. Here's part of an adult's account of a shopping expedition:

Anyway, I got down there by about 10, and fortunately there wasn't much of a queue, otherwise I'd've had to wait for ages.

Actually, I found just what I was after, too, in the very first shop . . .

There are a number of important linking words in this extract which make the speech hang together and run smoothly – *anyway, and fortunately, otherwise, actually*, and *too*. Without them, the story would be awkward and disjointed.

I got down there by 10. There wasn't much of a queue. I'd've had to wait for ages. I found just what I was after . . .

There are hundreds of such linking words and phrases in English – *also, for example, at any rate, as a matter of fact, quite frankly, moreover, however, you know, I mean, they say, I'm afraid* . . . Adults put them into their speech and writing all the time. What about children?

Such connecting features are almost entirely absent from 5-year-old speech. These children connect sentences with *and* and a few other conjunctions (as we've seen in Chapter 5). But they don't go in for these more mature ways of linking sentences together. Admittedly, there are linguistically precocious 5-year-olds who manipulate items like *I'm afraid* with unselfconscious ease. Once, I even heard *however* emerge from the mouth of one such child. And Susie (in Chapter 1) was also sporadically precocious in this respect: in her 'three little pigs' story, you may recall, she used *you know what* and *let me see*. But most children don't start introducing such items until they're about seven. This dialogue was recorded in a classroom, for example:

Janet (6;10)is leaving the room
Teacher: Janet, where are you going?
Janet: Actually, I'm going to the toilet.

One of the few studies of the way in which children learn to build up stretches of connected speech was carried out by Cheryl Scott in 1984. She analysed samples of speech taken from 114 children aged 6 to 12 to see what linking words and phrases were in use. She found hardly any such items in the speech of 6-year-olds. There were 27 of these children, and in the sample they produced 3,700 utterances. But only 82 instances of linking items were found – *now, then, so, anyway, though,* and *really*.

By 8 years of age, the children were using an increasing range of linking words and the totals kept on increasing throughout the study. At older ages, not only were new words being used, but they were being used more frequently. Some of the 'older' linkers were *for instance, like, say, instead, anyhow, at least, actually, in fact, maybe, perhaps, probably, of course,* and *really*. The commonest words were still *now, then, so, anyway, though,* and *really*. But even at 12, the range and frequency of these words fell far short of what you'd expect to find when adults talk.

Here are some examples of how the children used these words in Scott's study. You'll hear plenty of similar examples in the speech of your own child at this age – but you have to listen carefully because they're often said very quickly, and it's easy to lose track of them in a stream of fluent speech.

> I wouldn't like to be a pig, though.
> Who do you have for English, then?
> Well, stick it in, then.
> So, we decided to take it apart . . .
> Now, does this look good enough?
> Not as far as I know, anyway.
> I watch amusing things, really.
> They like John Travolta, most probably.

Looking beneath the surface

Apart from learning some new grammatical structures, children also make other kinds of linguistic progress in their early school years. In particular, they learn to tell the difference between sentences that sound very similar, and which have been confusing them for some time.

One of the best-known examples of this confusion is the difference between sentences containing *ask* and those containing *tell*. Children often mix these verbs up, as the following conversation suggests.

Mother (*preparing dinner*): Michael, go and ask daddy if he wants potatoes for dinner this evening.

Michael (6;9) (*trots off to the other room, where his father is reading the paper, and says*): Daddy, mummy says there's potatoes for dinner.

Father: That's nice.

(*Later, everyone is eating dinner. There's a lull in the conversation, during which the father says:*)

Father: This is lovely, darling, but why don't we try it with rice instead of potatoes sometimes?

(*Icicles form across the dining table.*)

Mother: Well, yes, but you said you wanted potatoes.

Father: No, I didn't.

Mother: You did. I sent Michael to ask you, and you said you did.

Father: Well, I don't remember that.

Mother: Yes, he did. (*To Michael*) You did go, didn't you?

(*Michael nods.*)

Father: Well, I don't remember any such thing. I remember him saying something about potatoes, but he didn't ask me if I wanted any.

Mother: Well he should have done, because that's what I asked him to do. (*Turns to Michael.*) Why didn't you ask daddy like I told you?

Poor Michael. Trapped by his *ask/tell* problem and all because silly daddy happened to mention the rice. If daddy had kept his mouth shut, there'd have been no trouble.

That's the tricky thing about comprehension problems of this kind. Adults often don't notice that a child hasn't understood what was said to them, because it doesn't become a major issue. If the father had indeed said nothing, we would never have known that Michael was confusing the meaning of *ask* and *tell* at this point. How many other occasions were there, I wonder, when there were similar confusions, and no one noticed anything.

The same thing can happen with a child's use of vocabulary unless you take the trouble to check. Jane (8;0) was drawing a picture of some dinosaurs, and said *I've done a lovely brontosaurus.* Her mother came over to see and exclaimed 'That's not a brontosaurus, that's a stegosaurus – look, it's got spikes all down its back' (the mother was well into dinosaurs, having had to read her 10-year-old's school project on the subject some time before).

She was thus able to find out that Jane's understanding of dinosaur terminology wasn't very good. But imagine if she'd been busy with the ironing when Jane said her brontosaurus sentence, and she'd replied 'Yes, dear, very nice', without moving from the ironing board. She would never have known about Jane's misunderstanding.

In the course of a day, there must be hundreds of cases like this where children get things wrong and we never notice because we don't have time or opportunity to check. The surprising thing is that it doesn't seem to matter much. The children survive and learn the differences in the end. Doubtless wide reading, careful teaching and regular homework have a great deal to do with it.

But children don't get homework on such grammatical differences as *ask* and *tell*, so what is going on here? The problem arises out of the fact that sentences containing these words can look identical, on the surface. Compare:

> Ask John what time it is.
> Tell John what time it is.

In the 1960s, Carol Chomsky carried out a series of studies in which she tested children's ability to distinguish sentences of this kind. She found that 5-year-olds made no difference at all: everyone interpreted *ask* as if it meant *tell* – just like Michael in the story. Not until children were 9 was the distinction consistently made.

Not all uses of *ask* and *tell* are mastered as late as this, though. When these verbs are being used to get people to *do* something (rather than just to report on something), children seem to be aware of a difference between them much earlier. In 1981, Kathryn Bock and Mary Hornsby studied the way children between 3 and 6 spoke when they were instructed to 'ask' people and to 'tell' people. One group of children were told to 'ask' someone to pass them pieces of a puzzle. Another group were instructed to 'tell' someone to pass them the pieces. Bock and Hornsby found that the children's sentences gradually became more polite, when they were 'asking', and didn't become more polite when they were 'telling'. The word *please* seemed to be crucial, as you can see from the kinds of sentences they used:

'Askers'	*'Tellers'*
3-year-olds	3-year-olds
Give that cup to me.	I want that one.
Can I have the giraffe?	Can I have a piece?
6-year-olds	6-year-olds
Please can I have that lion?	Give me the giraffe.
Could I have one please, Dwayne?	Will you give me a piece, Brian.
Julie, may I have a piece?	Can I have a piece of the puzzle?

Ask and *tell* are not the only verbs which cause problems. Carol Chomsky looked at another pair of verbs in the same way: the distinction between *tell* and *promise*. Note the difference between these two sentences:

> David told John to go out.
> David promised John to go out.

The two sentences look the same but they mean very different things. In the first sentence, it is John who will go out. In the second sentence, it is David who will go out, assuming he keeps his promise.

Once again, children don't make this distinction at around age 5. You can find this out for yourself, by giving a 5-year-old the same kind of task as Chomsky did in her experiments. Take two of the child's favourite toys – Chomsky used Donald Duck and a clown called Bozo. Then give the child the following instructions:

Donald tells Bozo to hop across the table. You make him do it.

Afterwards, give the child this instruction:

Donald promises Bozo to do a somersault. You make him do it.

And see what happens.

You'll find that the child will make Bozo hop across the table, in the first case – and Bozo will also do the somersault, in the second case. In other words, *tell* will be understood correctly, but *promise* will not.

Chomsky explained her results in the following way. If there's any doubt as to which noun does the action, the child will choose the one nearest to the verb. This rule works well enough for most verbs in the language. There are just a few exceptions. *Promise* is one of these, so children will try to make it conform to the general rule. It takes them some time to learn that it's an exception. Once again, children are 8 or 9 before they work out what's going on – that the person making a promise is the one who has to carry it out.

Playing with language

There's another way in which children look beneath the surface of language, and that is when they start to play with language, in order to make jokes, puns, riddles and suchlike. It's probably the most dreaded period of language acquisition, as any parent knows who has had to put up with an interminable series of 'knock, knock' jokes, said with great seriousness by an 8-year-old. Here are some examples, to inform those who have not yet had this experience, and to remind those who would prefer to forget.

1. Waiter, what's this?
   It's bean soup.
   I don't care what it's *been*. What is it now?

2. What's five Q and five Q?
   Ten Q.
   You're welcome!

3. What did the mummy broom say to the baby broom?
   Go to sweep.

4. What would you do if someone stole a bottle of perfume?
   I'd put a detective on the scent.

5. Why was the thief caught stealing a trayful of watches?
   Because he took too much time.

6. Why can't two elephants go swimming at the same time?
   Because they've only got one pair of trunks.

7. What is at the end of everything?
   The letter G.

8. What kind of animal can jump higher than a house?
   Any animal. Houses can't jump.

These are typical of the thousands of jokes and riddles which are based on language. But they play with language in different ways. 1, 2, and 3 are based on sound-play. 4 and 5 play on the difference between an idiom and a literal meaning – with 4 additionally requiring a knowledge of spelling. 6 is based on an ambiguous word. 7 depends on shifting the listener's attention away from the meaning of the sentence to the way it is constructed. And 8 is based on two competing interpretations of the grammar of the sentence.

Go to sweep!! I can't go on! Enough to say that children do not usually show much understanding or appreciation of linguistic jokes before the age of 6. Then there's a period of a year or so while the joke slowly dawns on them – a period in which they infuriate older brothers and sisters by asking them to explain jokes they hear on television. By 8, they have mastered several of the simpler kinds of joke for themselves. But it is not until 10 or 11 that they have real control over the longer and more complex jokes (such as the 'Englishman, Irishman and Scotsman' type). Even so, at age 10, one study showed that less than 40 per cent of riddles told to children were fully comprehended. And another study showed that even if children could tell a joke, and laugh at it, there was no guarantee that they would be able to explain it to others. Here's an example, from a 1977 study by Barbara Fowles and Marcia Glanz:

> What dog keeps the best time?
> A watch dog.

Gillie (age 7) was asked to explain the joke:

Gillie: It's a dog that watches your house.
Adult: But why does it keep the best time?
Gillie: Because it's a *watch dog*! A *watch* dog!
Adult: I don't get it.
Gillie: Well I just can't explain it (*said with disgust*).

Six-year-olds were at an even greater loss. Noel could only say this, about one of the riddles:

Because ... because ... I think ... no, it couldn't be, no ...
I just don't remember.

And Fernando cited authority – referring to the adult who had
told the riddle:

She said it! She said that's the answer. That's why it's funny!

Talking about language

Discussing the meaning of jokes leads us towards a further important skill which children develop in the early years of school,
though they show several signs of it in the pre-school years. They
become able to talk *about* language.

Adults, of course, do a great deal of talking about language to
children, from around age three. Here is a selection of remarks
about language made by parents of pre-school children (the
language terms are in italics):

Don't *shout*.	Slow down, I can't *understand* you.
That *sounds* silly.	That's a clever thing to *say*!
What a pretty *voice*!	Shall I *write* your name on here?
That's a *big O*.	Don't *say* that *word*!
What's that *called*?	Shall I *tell* you a *story*?

It's not surprising, then, that children will pick up some of the
words which describe features of language. They're not quite up
to 'preposition' and 'past tense', but by 5 most children have
made considerable progress nonetheless. Here are some comments
from a 4-year-old:

O begins with orange.
X is for kisses.
I *done some letters* in playgroup.
We had a nice *story* in playgroup today.
I *writ my name* on there.
Help me, daddy, 'cos I'm difficult with *letters*.
Mummy, I can *say* 'gin and tonic'! (A genuine example,
I swear!)

Learning to read is of course the area which will bring up a
mass of technical terms – terms such as 'spelling', 'word', 'space',

'sentence', 'full-stop', 'capital letter', and of course all the letters of the alphabet. Most children will have met some of the letters before they go to school. Alphabet books go down very well as presents for pre-school children. And children aren't scared of giving their own opinions as to what letters and reading are all about, as you can see from such 'interpretations' as 'X is for kisses'. There are some more examples of this kind on p. 209.

There is even some awareness at 5 years of age of the vocal movements involved in speech. Branky Zei published a study in 1979 in which she reported what children aged 5 to 9 said when asked to say what they felt when they spoke, and pronounced certain sounds. They had quite definite views.

Adult: What do you feel when you say [s]?
Pierre (5;0): Tongue moves at the end.
Adult: What do you mean, 'at the end'?
Pierre: When we finish the talking, it goes in. It goes in and down also at the same time.
Adult: And what do you feel when you say [i]?
Pierre: The tip of the lips goes smiling.
Adult: Is that all?
Pierre: The tummy gets a tiny bit fatter.

'The tip of the lips goes smiling'! Marvellous. And by 9, there's even greater precision.

Adult: Suppose that I don't know how to say [t] and you want to teach me how to do it. Tell me what I must do to say [t].
Catherine (9;0): Well you have to touch the front part of your tongue at the top part of your mouth, and try and let out sound and then open your mouth and let it come out.

Using language

I've spent most of this book talking about the different sounds, words, and grammatical constructions which children learn over the first few years of life. I've not said much about the many situations in which they actually *use* these structures – whether at home, in the shops, in church, talking to their parents, talking to strangers, talking to other children, telling stories, playing games of pretend, and so on. You'll certainly notice many differences, as children extend their social horizons. If a situation is unfamiliar, they may not use their language as efficiently as they would in a familiar setting. And they'll gradually pick up different styles of speech for use in these different settings. These styles have been noted in children very early on, even at the beginning of the fourth year.

During the fifth year, they often arrive home (after a visit to a friend's house, or to playgroup) with an array of new words which often take parents by surprise. This is the time when they readily pick up other children's slang (words for going to the toilet, for instance), and they will often demonstrate an unexpected awareness of rude words. 'Sod the brick,' said Steven, as he dropped a brick on his foot. He was 4. His father swallowed hard, but he couldn't really complain, for that was his own curse he was hearing. Out of the mouths of babes . . .

Children at this age can pick up new pronunciations too. This is most noticeable if the family has moved from one part of the country to another, where there is a markedly different accent. A pure Lancashire accent can be infiltrated by Cockney in no time at all, at around 4½ years of age. Or vice versa. Parents may not like it, but they can't do a thing about it. From now on, children will copy their peer group rather than their parents, as far as accent is concerned.

But the most noticeable developments in children's ability to use their language come when the child makes the big break, and arrives in school. A whole new linguistic world opens up. There is no longer just 'English'. There is formal English, for use in the classroom, and informal English, for use in the playground. There is the language you use when speaking, and the very different language you use when writing. These are distinctions which children take a long time to appreciate.

Take writing, for instance. When children first develop enough skill to write a little story, they automatically write it as they would speak it. One result is an essay full of *ands* and 'empty' words, such as pronouns. Here's an example, from a 7-year-old (I have corrected the spelling):

It was my birthday and I got a car and I got a gun and a game and we had a party and a cake and he gave me a big jigsaw and I was very tired.

That was the whole story, by the way. In due course, this child will be taught not to join all his sentences together with *and*, and to avoid too many pronouns – especially ones where it isn't clear who is meant (such as *he*, in this example).

But apart from the basic distinction between speech and writing, school raises many other uses of language of a more specialized kind. There's the special language which accompanies number work, with all its technical terms (sets, graphs, add, subtract . . .) and special instructions. There's the language of assembly, with its careful reading and careful listening. There's the language of school reading books, which can range from the delightful to the bizarre ('Look, John, look. See the boat.') Religious language may be encountered for the first time – or a different kind of religious language from what the child has been used to. And as children move higher up the school, so these specialized languages proliferate. Science, history, geography, cooking, and many other subjects appear, with their new words and styles.

Parents may take some time to get used to their child's new-found, alien linguistic behaviour during this period, especially when all kinds of local child slang and jargon arrive home along with the schoolbooks. Some of the new language can be truly fascinating – such as the rhymes young children use when they play, or the intricate technical distinctions which are drawn between different kinds of marble. Some of it can also provoke disapproval – such as the impolite forms they acquire for arguing, or the use of a wide range of slang expressions.

Many parents at this stage find themselves insisting on two standards – 'You can talk like that with your friends, but not in the house!' This is only natural. A certain amount of well-timed, tolerant parental correction and comment is an important part of general education, as the child comes to learn about the standards and expectations of the adult world. It does children no service, in the long run, if they receive no guidance about linguistic standards from their parents. However, too rigid, unsympathetic, or pedantic an approach is just as undesirable. The parent who corrects *every* instance of children's colloquial pronunciation, grammar, or vocabulary is focusing too much attention on language, and this can be at the expense of life. An 8-year-old child once came home full of the day's experience. 'Mummy, mummy, guess what, we got a new teacher, and –' The parent interrupted. 'No, listen, Jane, I've told you before, don't say *got*, say *have* . . .' Result: one deflated child and a shared experience lost.

This is an area where there is no scientific guidance. How people behave will be governed by their backgrounds, personalities and parental intuitions. At one extreme, there are parents who are tolerant of all usage – for example, permitting their children to swear, or call adults by their first names. At the other extreme, there are the linguistic disciplinarians, prescribing a narrow language path, and coming down hard when a child wanders away from it. Faced with this enormous range of attitudes, the only advice is common-sense: to aim for a balance between correcting and taking no notice and, when intervention is felt to be needed, to explain why one form is preferred over another. 'That's the way we talk when we're being polite . . . being careful . . . on our best behaviour . . .' In this way, parental guidance is more likely to make a positive contribution to the developing linguistic awareness of the child.

To conclude

So, then, with all this progress and developing awareness, can we finally say that, after the early school years, the process of language acquisition has come to an end? Yes and no.

In one sense, we have to recognize that language learning never ends. The vocabulary level of the pre-adolescent child must be somewhere between 10,000 and 20,000 words – but this is only a fraction of the total vocabulary of the language, which is lurking silently in the wings. There are over a million words in English. Of course, few speakers ever master more than about a tenth of this total. The remainder is taken up by the enormous number of technical and regional terms, which only small numbers of people ever learn. But still, a tenth of a million is a lot of words. Whether you're 9 or 90 years old, there's always vocabulary to learn. It pays, some say, to increase your word power.

Moreover, there are always new linguistic worlds to discover – an extension of the stylistic explorations begun in the junior school. There are always new styles to appreciate, and some of them may need to be mastered if life is to be a success. Radio and television are a major source of new experiences in this respect – newsreading, commentary, discussions, parliamentary procedure, American vs British English ... Travel is another, bringing a close encounter with all kinds of new accents and dialects. And the vast field of written literature guarantees an ongoing encounter with fresh language use, for all who wish to read it.

When the child gets a job (or perhaps it should be 'if' these days), there will be a host of new usages to master – not just the technical jargon which goes with the job, but the language associated with the many situations which form the work environment – safety regulations, union rules, committee-speak, insurance forms, tax returns and much more. When adult hobbies and leisure pursuits come along, they will be seen to have their linguistic side too. There is probably as much jargon in bird-watching as in chemical engineering. And for those who join an amateur dramatic group, even long-standing habits of pronunciation can be made to change.

But in another sense, language acquisition *is* over, as the child approaches adolescence. There are no more sounds to learn: all the vowels and consonants of the native accent have been in use for some time. And all bar a tiny fraction of the grammatical constructions have been learned. If someone's language were suddenly to stop developing at about age 13, they would have little difficulty in surviving, linguistically speaking, for the rest of their lives. There's not enough to be said, to justify another chapter, on the later school years. You can leave well alone, now. No more diaries. The rest is silence.

Feature 19 | It ain't what you say . . .

Intonation – the melody of language – is one of the first features to be heard in the emerging speech of a child towards the end of the first year (see p. 45). But when children start using intonation to express their meaning, they don't learn all the possible tones of voice immediately. In fact, 10 years later they're still trying to sort out all the different nuances of meaning conveyed by the adult voice.

One of the first studies to show this was published by Alan Cruttenden in 1974. He started with the well-known melodic differences which can be heard whenever radio or TV announcers read the results of a football match. The way British announcers do it, it's quite possible to predict the result before the second score is read out – whether it will be a draw, a home win or an away win.

In each case, the first team, and its score, is read out with a melody which rises to quite a high level. You can't predict anything at the point when the announcer says

Liverpool   3

But as soon as the name of the second team is read out, you know straight away what the result is, even though you haven't heard the score yet.

– For a draw, the pitch of the voice usually falls from quite high up to quite low down in the voice range. The emphasis is on the team's name, and the actual score tags on at the end, also very low down in pitch, and not strongly stressed at all. It's as if the voice is saying: 'The second score doesn't do anything special – it's the same as the first – so I'm not going to draw special attention to it.' If we drew this on a kind of musical stave, it would look like this. (Each black dot marks a syllable, and the lines mark noticeable glides in pitch.)

```
              Liverpool    3      Everton    3
High up       _____
                                    ⌐
              •  •  •       ⌐‾     \
Low down                            \  •     •
              _____
```

– A home win has a very different pattern. Here the second part of the result is usually uttered in a much lower tone, with the actual score being said more loudly. It looks like this:

```
              Liverpool    3      Everton    2
              _____
              •  •  •       ⌐‾     •  •  •
                                            ⌐‾
              _____
```

This time the voice is saying: 'There *is* a different score coming up, so I'll draw attention to it – but, sadly, it isn't as big as the first.'
– An away win presents yet another pattern. Here the second part of the result is usually said in a much higher tone than the first, with the score being quite strongly emphasized. It looks like this:

```
              Liverpool    3      Everton    4
              _____
                                            \
              •  •  •       ⌐‾     •  •  •    \
              _____
```

The voice is now saying: 'There's a new score coming, everyone, and wow, it's bigger than the first one.'

Cruttenden drew up a list of possible games, such as Forfar vs Stranraer. He chose Scottish teams because he was studying children from the Manchester area and he didn't want to use well-known English teams in case this influenced the children's judgements. Some children can't bear the thought of their favourite team losing, and that would mess up any experiment.

He recorded the results using a typical announcer intonation, but left the second score out – for instance,

```
              Forfar       3      Stranraer
              _____
                                   \
              •  •          ⌐‾      \
                                     \  •
              _____
```

It must have sounded as if the announcer had been murdered at the crucial moment!

He then played the recording to a group of adults, all mother-tongue speakers of English, and asked them to guess the overall result – draw, home or away. They all predicted the result correctly.

Now the stage was set for the children. Cruttenden played the tape to 28 boys in the junior classes of a primary school. The children were aged between 7 and 11. He gave them a few practice examples first, to show them what they had to do. What were *their* guesses like?

Five of the children didn't seem to grasp the point of the experiment. In every case they gave the same result – all home wins or all away wins! Fortunately, the remainder were more cooperative!

There were three 7-year-olds in the group: they scored an average of 3 correct out of 7 results. There were twelve 8-year-olds: their score was an average of 3·2 correct. The ten 9-year-olds scored 4·1; and the two 10-year-olds scored 4·5. There was thus a clear development in the ability to interpret the intonation patterns.

But something else is more significant. Even at age 10, the children hadn't reached the level of competence shown by the adults. Only one child in the whole group got all seven results correct (he was 8;11). Only eight children scored over 4. Most of them did quite well in identifying draws (15 made no errors here), but the other patterns were quite erratic.

Cruttenden's children were all boys. I tried out the same experiment informally on some girls once and the results were the same. No sexism here.

Nor does interest in football have anything to do with it. Cruttenden actually rated the children for their interest in football. Some were keen. Others weren't. There was a weak correlation: the more you're interested in football (and thus, presumably, listen to the scores on radio or TV), the better you'll do. But this doesn't explain all the results. In fact, the child who did best was rated as having no interest in football at all!

Now, if this experiment told us only about how children come to understand football results, it wouldn't be very interesting. But the patterns of intonation which the announcer uses in giving the results are found in everyday conversation as well. For instance, if someone says:

Has John bought a blue car or a red car?

the intonation bounces along just as it does in a score-draw result:

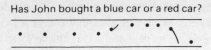

Has John bought a blue car or a red car?

The voice is saying: 'The second mention of the word *car* doesn't add any new information – it's the same as the first – so I'm not going to draw special attention to it. Pay attention to the colours instead.'

It very much looks, then, as if children are still sorting out the meanings of intonation patterns as late as 9 or 10 years of age, or even older. Other tests of intonation produce similar results. For instance, do you think that 10-year-olds would be able to tell the difference between the following pairs of sentences?

She dressed, and fed the baby (i.e. the mother got dressed, and then she fed the baby).
She dressed and fed the baby (i.e. the baby was dressed and fed).

In writing, you can make the difference by using a comma. In speech, the two sentences sound quite different. Say them aloud (unless you're reading this in a train, and can't!). In the first, you'll pause at the comma and your voice will go up. In the second, you'll read straight through and your voice will go down.

In a 1985 study Cruttenden gave this pair of sentences to 20 adults and 20 children, showing them three pictures. In the first picture, a mother is putting her dress on, with a feeding bottle ready. In the second picture, she's dressing the baby, with the feeding bottle in the background. In the third picture (which was included as a distraction), she's feeding herself. Everyone had to point to one of the pictures when they heard each sentence.

Once again, the results were clear. On the second sentence, for instance, 19 out of 20 adults made the correct decision, whereas only 9 out of 20 children did. Several other sentences, showing other differences in intonation, were also tested, and the results were on similar lines. However, the adults themselves didn't always achieve good scores, suggesting that the task was quite a difficult one to grasp.

Here's an easy intonation contrast which you can try out for yourself. Find some 8-year-olds and say you're going to ask them a simple question after they hear some sentences. Give them an irrelevant question first, so that they get the idea (such as *Michael gave a pencil to Fred. Who gave the pencil to Fred?*). Then give them the first relevant sentence (saying it with a strong emphasis on the words in italics):

John gave a book to *Jim*, and he gave one to *Mary*.

You then ask:

Who gave the book to Mary?

And the children will reply 'John' – along with various expressions of contempt, that you should be asking such ridiculously simple questions.

Next, say the same sentence, but with a different emphasis (making sure the *he* is particularly well stressed):

John gave a book to *Jim*, and *he* gave one to *Mary*.

Again you ask:

Who gave the book to Mary?

This time, the answer should be 'Jim'. But you'll find that most 8-year-olds will still say 'John'. And even 9-year-olds can be caught out. They assume that the first person in the sentence is the one who does the action. They haven't learned to appreciate that a strong emphasis on some other word can change the meaning of a sentence quite dramatically.

There's no doubt that as children approach secondary school, they still have a lot to learn about the meanings conveyed by the inflection of the adult voice. I wonder if they pick up all the nuances in the speech of their teachers, for instance? If not, they could always be set some extra weekend homework: obligatory listening to the football results!

Feature 20 | Talking backwards

It's a game, of course – but *what* a game! The rules are simple. You have to pronounce every word with the sounds in reverse order. And then you speak as fast as you can! It's something that just a few children do – but not before 7.

What does it sound like, exactly? In 1981, Nelson Cowan and Lewis Leavitt published a study of two boys aged 8;10 and 9;11, each of whom had (quite independently) invented a game of talking backwards and apparently without anyone's help. Both children had normal forwards speech. When they were recorded, they'd both been using backwards speech for about a year. The researchers asked each child to 'translate' 100 words into backwards speech, and also a few sentences.

The two children turned out to be very different. There seem to be two distinct 'styles' of talking backwards. The first child (A) reversed the *sounds* in each word, and ignored the spelling. The second (B) reversed the *spellings*, sounding the letters out. The resulting pronunciations sounded very different. *Size*, for example, would come out as [zais], using A's method, but would come out as [ezis], using the second.

Here are some of the words they spoke (in a simplified transcription):

	Child A	Child B
nine	nain	enin
guy	aig	jag
boil	loib	ljab
mouse	saum	esuam
continue	ujenitnak	utenik
bomb	mab	bmab
castle	lesak	eltsak
axe	ska	ksa
bone	nob	enob
auto	ota	otuwa
inhale	leni	elena
elevate	tevele	etalevet

Some quite complicated words were produced in this way, such as (from A)

automobile libomota
elementary iritnemele

The sentence 'Please present an idea to the class' was translated by B in the following way (the italics mark the rhythm):

eselp te*ne*zep na *ed*e at ete *selk*.

You'll have noticed that the words aren't always perfectly accurate reversals. The children have introduced their own short cuts. But they are certainly following a system of rules, when they talk like this. They're not randomly guessing.

Cowan and Leavitt read several sentences out to the children, taking an average of 2·04 seconds to say each one. When the children repeated them, in backwards speech, they took much longer. A's average time was 6·51 seconds; B's was 4·06.

Why do they do it? Talking backwards is one of a large number of language games which children invent at around this age. They probably stem from the same kind of creative joy which they show in jokes and riddles, which also emerge around age 7 (as we've seen, p. 185). Many of the games involve the invention of a 'secret' language – one which won't be understood by adults, or by children from outside your own group. But there are only so many ways of inventing a new language on the basis of the one you already speak, so it's not surprising that the same kind of thing turns up all over the world. Children speak backwards in other languages too.

Do children lose the ability when they grow up? It seems not. Cowan and Leavitt interviewed 27 adults who had all been backwards talkers as children. Most had begun around 8–10 years of age; but a few had begun in adolescence. They were still able to talk backwards, though some were only able to do it slowly, and some could do it only on quite short words. However, three of these adults didn't just reverse the order of the sounds in words: they reversed the order of the words in sentences as well – and often at speeds very similar to those found in forwards speech! Who knows? There may be a backwards-talking Olympics one day.

One of the most important skills children have to learn is how to define words by using other words. It's not something they have to do very much before they get to school, but once in school you can't survive without it, especially in the junior years.

So how do children learn to define? Bonnie Litowitz published a study in 1977 which suggested that there are five levels which children go through when they are asked 'What's X?' or 'What does X mean?'

Level 1 The most primitive stage is when the children don't reply at all. They simply gesture at X, if they can see it, or act it out in some way. Alternatively, they use an 'empty' word, such as *that* or *this*, while making a gesture:

Adult: What's *snap*?
Child: Like this (*makes a gesture*).

Level 2 Children give back a word which is related in meaning to the one they've been asked to define, but they don't say anything about the link between the two. It's a very ambiguous, telegraphic response.

Adult: What's wrong?
Child: Sock.

Adult: What's a bicyle?
Child: The man, a lady.

Level 3 Here children give back more information, but it takes the form of an example from the child's own experience. The definition is thus an idiosyncratic one. It might work for the child but not necessarily for anyone else.

Adult: What's a clock?
Child: When it rings it's time to wake and eat and get dressed and go to school.

Adult: What's a bicycle?
Child: You ride on and you fall off.

Sometimes the word is repeated in the reply:

Adult: What's a diamond?
Child: People steal – diamonds.

And sometimes just one or two features of the word's meaning are given in reply:

Adult: What's an umbrella?
Child: It's black.

Adult: What's a bicycle?
Child: You could use it to ride to Bruce's –not always in the street.

Level 4 Here, children are becoming aware that word meanings are shared by others. They stop defining words in a purely personal way and try to say things which are generally true. Often, their answers begin with 'When you . . .' or 'You could . . .', at this stage. As with the previous stage, they seem to stress the *functions* which objects perform, rather than the physical features of the objects (whether they're round, long, and so on):

Adult: What's a knife?
Child: A knife is when you cut with it.

Adult: What's a nuisance?
Child: When people are bad.

Level 5 The final stage is the 'proper' definition of a word, which takes the form 'An X is a kind of Y which has the features Z'. For example, if asked to define *chair*, adults would probably say something like: 'A chair is a piece of furniture which has four legs and a back, and you sit on it.' In Litowitz's study, none of the children she was using (from age 4;5 to 7;5) produced any definitions of this kind. But there were a few definitions which came near:

Adult: What's a shoe?
Child: A thing you put on your foot.

Adult: What's a donkey?
Child: An animal.

At an older age, you're likely to hear definitions such as these:

Adult: What's an apple?
Child (9;0): It's a sort of fruit, and it's round, and green or red, and it grows on trees, and we eat it.

And at a still older age – presumably after much practice in school – they will be able to produce definitions like this:

Adult: What's a bus?
Child (13;6): A bus is a vehicle which has lots of seats and carries passengers for money.

It's not far from here to the world of the professional definers – the people who write our dictionaries. And the moral is plain. If you want children to make progress in using and understanding definitions, get them a simple dictionary, and help them to use it. They'll be able to cope from around 7 or 8 years of age.

Feature 22 | As big as . . .

All the best forms of verbal art rely on images. Poets startle us with their vivid comparisons, and the unexpected associations they make between words. Shakespeare compares life to – a candle. A heart to – a red rose. When do children learn that they too can be poets in their own small way?

A team of American child language researchers led by Howard Gardner reported the results of a study of this topic in 1975. They were interested in finding out how children developed their ability to use figures of speech. They therefore asked over 100 children – some pre-schoolers, and some aged 7, 11, 14 and 19 – to complete a sentence with a figure of speech. They told the child a short 'story', which always ended with an unfinished sentence. The child had to finish it off. For example, one story went like this:

We're glad to have you at this party for our son. Look at that boy standing over there. He looks as gigantic as –

The stories included a wide range of adjectives, such as *as soft as . . ., as happy as . . .,* and *as bright as . . .*

Here are some of the endings produced by each age-group:

Pre-school children Most endings were short and conventional. They often referred to people. Sometimes they were confused.

cold as snow	tall as you
tall as a giant	happy as Elizabeth
warm as snow.	

But several children were able to produce some quite interesting endings, even at this age:

quiet as a magic marker	soft as a rainbow
sad as a pimple	stony as a stupid person.

In fact, this group produced far more original, interesting endings than children at any other age! In some cases, this was probably because they didn't know exactly how to use a word in the first place. Some interesting usages would be bound to turn up as a result of guesswork. On the other hand, many of the instances suggested that these children really could appreciate the force of a novel figure of speech.

Seven-year-olds This was a very literal-minded group, preferring concrete comparisons, and not going in much for imaginative endings.

> soft as a pillow　　bright as the sky.

Eleven-year-olds This group had a strong preference for the expected, conventional ending, but they weren't as literal-minded as the 7-year-olds. The comparisons were generally concrete, and often made use of personal names:

> tall as Wilt Chamberlain　　hard as stale bread.

Sometimes, a comparison was embellished in some way:

> strong as a gigantic boulder sticking in the ground.

Older children Most of this group took a conventional ending, and elaborated it in some way, often quite vividly:

> warm as a summer's night in Montana
> boiling as hot lava coming down a mountain volcano
> thundering as the President making a speech on television.

And yet, they sometimes made quite inappropriate comparisons:

> hard as rubber　　stony as clay.

A few used endings which approached the poetic:

> colours as light as an old folk tune
> colours as bright as pomegranates in a coal mine.

But on the whole there was a reluctance to use figures of speech which mixed different kinds of experience. Some of this group even insisted that it wasn't possible to compare a colour with a sound, or feeling with hearing. No future poets here.

The research team also compiled a set of their own figures of

speech, and asked the children which ones they liked best, and why. They distinguished four kinds:
– a very literal type of comparison, such as *as gigantic as the most gigantic person in the whole world*;
– a fairly literal-minded, conventional comparison, such as *as gigantic as a skyscraper in the centre of town*;
– a more interesting, appropriate comparison, such as *as gigantic as a double-decker cone in a baby's hand*;
– an inappropriate comparison, such as *as gigantic as a clock from a department store*.

Again, there was an interesting development. The youngest children had no particular preferences. They sometimes chose an appropriate ending, sometimes an inappropriate one. *As tall as string* was quite common, suggesting that they weren't entirely sure of how *tall* is used in English (see p. 123).

At seven, the children preferred the very literal endings, and gave concrete reasons for their choice:

I chose 'warm as toast' because it gets real hot in the toaster.
The face of the prison guard is stony, because the prison has stone walls.

Some gave personal reasons:

I chose 'light as a feather' because I like feathers.

Eleven-year-olds preferred the less literal, conventional endings. One child rejected a very literal ending, saying 'that doesn't say anything new'. They also didn't like the more figurative endings, making such remarks as 'an ice cream cone isn't gigantic' or 'a colour can't be loud'. But a few children seemed to be more aware. One child gave a lovely reason for her preference:

The tree is sad because it's the last day of autumn, and there is no one else around.

The oldest groups liked the more figurative endings, and went into the basis of the comparison in much more detail:

Usually an ice cream cone isn't that big, but in the hands of a little child I guess it would be gigantic.
A splash of red can be thundering because it breaks out noisily in the centre of the paper.

Both parts of the study – the children's productions as well as their preferences – showed a steady development as the children got older, much as we might expect. But there was a general reluctance to produce the more striking figures of speech, at any age. Whether this was due to the novelty of the task, or to a more deep-rooted fear of making unconventional, novel comparisons isn't at all clear. If it's the latter, it must be something children pick up as they get older. There was certainly no sign of this caution in the 5-year-olds! Perhaps we're all poets at heart, after all.

What do children know *about* language?

We've seen that learning to talk about language is an important step in a child's later development (p. 187), though they show some signs of this ability from around age 3. In particular, they need to have a good command of language terms in order to cope with the task of learning to read. Here are some ways in which you can find out what they know, during the pre-reading period. Most of the tasks are taken from a research study by Emilia Ferreiro and Ana Teberosky, using children between 4 and 6 years of age, which was first published in English in 1983.

Remember that if you try out these tasks, you're not trying to *teach* the child anything. You're simply wanting to find out what they know. Naturally, they won't know much to begin with. But gradually, you'll find that they become more aware of what is going on in reading and writing – long before they actually learn to read. Ferreiro and Teberosky's book is in fact called *Literacy Before Schooling*.

1. See if they know what 'reading' is. Show them a set of pictures of people doing different things – somebody reading a paper, looking at a painting, watching the buses go by and so on. Ask 'Who is reading?' or 'Who is doing some reading?' In the fourth year, they probably won't be able to tell the difference.

2. See if they know what 'writing' is. Show them pictures of people drawing, writing, painting a wall and so on. Once again, younger children will not be able to distinguish the language activity from the others.

3. See if they can tell the difference between pictures and print. One can be read and the other can't. Choose a few pictures and a few printed extracts, mix them up, and then ask 'Which can you read?'. Young children won't make a distinction. Everything which involves looking at a book is 'reading', whether there's language there or not.

4. Do they know which way round you read a page of print?

Ask them to show you how someone reads. They have to put their finger on the page and move it along to show you what people are doing when they're reading. Some young children go all over the place. Some start at the bottom of a page and move upwards. Some go from left to right; some from right to left. Some will even go in alternate directions, following the first line from left to right, then dropping down to the next line, and following that back from right to left. Some ancient Greek writing was like this – so they're not being so silly.

5. See if they know what a 'word' is. Show them cards on each of which you've written a single word. The words should be of different lengths – such as *a*, *go*, *cat*, *have*, *place*. Ask them, simply, without any explanation, 'Is this a word?' or 'Could this be a word?'. Ferreiro and Teberosky found that if a word had less than three letters in it, many children at around age 4 didn't accept that it could be a word. 'It's too small,' said one child, faced with the word *go*.

But even if a word has several letters in it, children will probably reject it if all the letters are the same. You can try this out by showing them a card with *mmmm* or *aaaaa*, and asking if they could be words. The answer will probably be no. To count as a word, it seems, the letters have to be different.

6. Can they tell the difference between letters and numbers? Take some blank cards, and write either a number or a letter on each. Mix them up and ask 'Which ones are letters?', 'Which ones are numbers?'. See if the children can sort them out. Most 4-year-olds can't.

7. Can they tell the difference between a letter and a punctuation mark? Ask them and see, using the same kind of card techniques. Put a full stop, a question mark and a pair of inverted commas on different cards, and mix them up with a few cards containing single letters. Young children will probably call all of them letters.

8. Do they know the names of letters? Many parents ask for this kind of information, especially when they're going through an alphabet book with the child. But a child who knows that 'A is for apple' may not be able to recognize the letter outside the setting of the alphabet book.

What you'll notice is that some letters stand a better chance of being recognized than others. Most children will recognize the first letter of their own first name. 'B is for Ben,' said one 4-year-old. 'J is for Julie,' said another. 'M for mummy' and 'D for daddy' are often known. X is for kisses, or for Xmas. K is often for Kelloggs (if the child has had years of staring at the back of cornflakes packets at breakfast time). In the Ferreiro and Teberosky study, which was carried out in South America, one of the most frequently recognized letters was Z. Z stood for Zorro – a popular television character, at the time!

7 | Complications?

Being bilingual

'And what will happen to *my* child?', you might be asking, if you happen to be a reader with a foreign spouse. One worried parent wrote like this: 'I am French, and married to an English husband. We live in England, and we have just had our first child. I want to speak French to her, but my husband can only speak English. What should we do? We don't want to confuse the child . . .' This view is very widely held. If children are exposed to more than one language at an early age, they will become confused. They'll mix up the languages and speak neither well. They'll fall behind in school. They'll ⊢

Enough of this gloom! There's no reason for it. The world is full of children who grow up bilingual without a linguistic care in the world. I mean that literally. Well over half the children in the world grow up in a multilingual environment. Traditionally, that hasn't been the case in Britain and the USA, so we're not so used to it. Most children in these two countries are monolingual. But as you travel around Europe, Africa, South Asia, China . . ., you'll find that we are the exception rather than the rule. There are millions of children who know two – or even three or more – languages, and thrive on it. They are certainly not delayed or disadvantaged by their bilingualism. On the contrary, their ability to handle more than one language can prove to be a real asset.

Let's return to the French/English situation, and see why there won't be a problem here either. The mother is probably thinking that her child will hear so much French and so much English at the same time that there's bound to be a muddle. But it won't be like that. Children aren't usually exposed to 50 per cent of one language and 50 per cent of another, during the first years of life. Usually, the mother is in far more contact with the child (see p. 54),

"*I write children's first readers.*
I drink
I smoke
I drink and smoke and write children's first readers
        I see your glass
        Your glass is empty
        I drink and smoke and write children's first readers and I
                see your glass is empty."

and that means the linguistic environment will be largely a monolingual one. Sometimes, the amount that a father says to his child, during the first year, can be as little as a tenth of what the child hears from the mother.

Even when a child *is* exposed to two languages equally, there's no problem. Throughout this book, I've been emphasizing the remarkable skill children have when they learn a language – in particular, the speed at which they operate. The same skills are found when there are two languages to be learned. By the end of the fourth year, in fact, most bilingual children have reached the same stage of linguistic development *in both languages* as have their monolingual counterparts.

But the process of learning two languages isn't exactly the same as the process of learning one. There seem to be at least three main stages of development. At first, the child builds up a list of words, just like a monolingual child does, but the list contains words from both languages. However, children at this stage don't act like adult translators. It's very rare for them to have words in this list which are equivalents in the two languages. After all, why should they? If they learn *baby* in English, what need is there to learn it additionally in French? Once they've learned it, they've learned it. (You have to think of this from the *children's* point of view. *They* don't know that the mother and father are speaking different languages!)

As a result of this simultaneous learning, the next step in development is an interesting one. When bilingual children start to make two-word sentences, they usually put words from the different languages together into the same sentence. Here are some examples from a German/English bilingual child of 2:

ein big cow ('a big cow') from up in Himmel ('sky')
alle Auto on the ship ('all car') er geht up ('he goes up')

At a somewhat later age, this child produced the following gem:

Mother: Don't you speak English any more?
Child: Nein. German.

The amount of vocabulary mixing rapidly declines, however. In one study, at the beginning of the third year, the amount of

mixing was between 20 per cent and 30 per cent; but by the end
of the third year it was less than 5 per cent.

Gradually, as the mixing dies away, children build up vocabulary in the two languages. After a while, they possess a large
number of equivalent words. But although they may have two
distinct vocabularies, they don't at this stage seem to have two
distinct grammars. The same types of sentence turn up, regardless
of which language the vocabulary belongs to. If one language has
adjectives going before nouns, and the other language has nouns
going before adjectives, children ignore the difference, and make
both languages work in the same way.

The final stage is one where the child speaks two languages,
which differ in sounds, grammar and vocabulary. They now know
the names of the languages, and are aware that they are not the
same. They use each language to the parent who speaks it, and
not to the other parent. Indeed, if one parent uses the language of
the other to the child, the child may be quite surprised or embarrassed, may not understand, may think it's a huge joke, or get
very upset. Virginia Volterra and Traute Taeschner reported
several such cases in a 1978 study of bilingual acquisition:

An Italian friend talks to Lisa (3;6) in German. Lisa
immediately becomes upset and begins to cry. The mother
tries to calm her, and says *Virginia spricht Deutsch* ('Virginia
speaks German'). Lisa slaps her mother.

At 3;11, Lisa's Italian father uses a short German sentence to her,
to which she immediately reacts:

Lisa: No, non puoi. ('No, you can't')
Father: Ich auch . . . spreche Deutsch. ('I also speak German')
Lisa: No, tu non puoi! ('No, you cannot')

It's also at this point that children start to play parents off
against each other, deliberately speaking in French to a monolingual English father, for example. One child would always
switch into French when he saw his English father approach
him meaningfully at bedtime!

There have now been several studies of bilingual language
acquisition and the message is loud and clear. There's no cause

for concern if parents treat their children in a normal, sensible way, talking to them in the way which comes most naturally and not getting self-conscious or contrived. Above all, it's not necessary to develop a complicated language-teaching policy – something which can happen when both parents are fluent in both languages. I've been told of one family who were so anxious to promote equal facility in their child that they worked out a timetable – English on Mondays, Welsh on Tuesdays, and so on. Of course they couldn't keep it up, but the home situation became quite tense for a while, until they dropped the idea.

Now *there's* a danger. There's a real risk of children being disturbed and muddled if parents try to impose a language learning regime on them that is beyond their capacity to understand. This often happens when the parents speak a language which is in danger of dying, or when they are immigrants. They may even refuse to allow the outside language into the house, because they're so anxious to maintain their mother tongue. I've seen such policies extend to the banning of school friends from the house, or the refusal to allow the child to watch television programmes in the outside language. Obviously, young children won't understand what is going on. And the risk is that the confusion and anxiety which follows may, ironically, affect their language learning ability. I've heard of one incident where a child simply stopped talking, as a result of the rigid line adopted by his parents. I'm sure it isn't an isolated case.

Being a twin

Most people have heard of the way twins sometimes develop a secret language of their own. A pair of American twins became world-renowned when they were heard to communicate in this way. They were headline news for a while, and a film was even made about them ('Poto and Cabengo', so-called because of the pet names they used for each other in this language). In fact, when the 'language' was analysed, it turned out to be based on English after all, a fact which was obscured by the speed at which the children spoke and by the idiosyncratic pronunciation which they developed.

Twins often develop a private form of communication. Indeed, it would be surprising if they didn't, because their language learning environment is unique. Where else would you find two children of exactly the same age, and probably at the same stage of linguistic development, with so much time together? Imagine the situation at night, when the babbling stage is developing. They're in the same room. It's dark and there's nothing to do except listen to the noises around. Across the room comes the sound of one child's babbling. What more natural than to respond to it? And, after a while, mightn't these babbling exchanges develop into something meaningful, and rather different from normal language?

Elinor Keenan found a great deal of language play in the early morning conversations of her twins. She recorded them when they were 2;9 and found long stretches of 'dialogue', in which each twin responded to the features of pronunciation it noticed in the other. Here's one such sequence:

Twin A: zaki su.
Twin B (*laughing*): zaki su zaki su (*both laugh*) aa
(*laughing*)
A: apii.
B: olp olt olt.
A: opii opii.
B: apii apii (*laughing*) api api api.
A: ai ju.
B. (*laughing*) ai ju api (*repeated several times*) (*laughs*) kaki.
A: ai ii oo.
B: ai ii o oo.

And so on. They are plainly enjoying themselves, and it's interesting to see how one child picks up some of the sounds of the other child and plays with them, before the other child does the same. Adults listening in might think that here we have a secret language – but it's no more than a piece of nonsense play – a game of phonetic tennis.

At other times, the dialogues are more intelligible, involving an enormous amount of repetition, along with changes of emphasis (marked by italics below):

A: You *silly*. You *silly*.

B: *No*, Toby's silly.
A: You *silly*. You *silly*.
B: No. *You* silly. No not, *you* silly.
A: *You* silly.
B: No. Not. *No* silly. *No* silly.
A: *No* silly.

The dialogue continues in this way for a further 38 exchanges!

But perhaps the most interesting feature of twin language is the way in which they 'share' the response to an adult question. Here's an example:

Mother: What can you see in the picture (*showing a picture of a cat and a dog*).
Twin A: A cat.
Twin B: And a dog.

Sometimes, these sequences run together very rapidly, with even quite short utterances being split in two:

Twin A: Puss.
Twin B: In boots.

Observers have been struck by the intuitive way in which one twin is able to respond so rapidly to what the other has just said, and how the second twin is able to anticipate when to stop. They don't talk at the same time very often. This skill can only come from the frequent opportunities the twins have had to talk together, in the early years. They know each other's rhythms and moods, and each is able to predict a great deal of what the other will say.

It's commonly said that twins are late in developing language, and this is true. They begin to speak later than single children, their sentences are shorter and less complex, their pronunciation is less mature, and so on. When the language of twins is formally assessed, during the third and fourth years, they are often found to be about 6 months behind the 'norm'. On the other hand, there are aspects of their language development which are ahead of single children – in particular, their ability to interact with adults, and to keep a conversation going. Moreover, if we were to measure the twins together, a much more advanced picture would emerge. Here's a sequence which illustrates this point.

Twin A: Got car.
Twin B: Big red car.
Twin A: In a garage.
Twin B: With a driver.

The children each seem to be at the two/three word stage of development, but is this entirely fair to them? As a 'team', they are producing a sentence which is 10 words long: 'Got big red car in a garage with a driver'.

Of course, they can't go on collaborating for ever. They need to develop independent lives. By 5, most twins have begun this process in language, as in other aspects of behaviour. Measures of twins' language at around 7 or 8 years of age show no important differences from the language of single children. They've caught up.

Language delay

There's so much individual variation among children that all ages mentioned in this book, as I said at the beginning, have to be taken with a pinch of salt. Thus there's no cause for concern if your child hasn't begun to produce some first words by twelve months, or has reached 2 and is still not joining words together into single sentences. I know of many cases of children who have been virtually silent until 2, and who have then begun to speak with a vengeance. The ages in this book are averages, guidelines, no more.

On the other hand, the averages do mean something. If most children are producing first words by twelve months and your child still hasn't produced a word six months later, then it's only natural to feel anxious. Other parents will be proudly talking about what their children are saying, and you will feel out of it. The best advice I can offer is to say, if you do feel anxious, talk about it – to whoever will listen. Compare your experiences with those of other parents. After you've heard a mother of seven say that 'two of hers didn't talk till 3', or words to that effect, you'll feel a bit better.

But what if time goes by, and there's still no sign of progress? Sooner or later you'll want to ask for a professional opinion. The first port of call is your health visitor or family doctor. After all, language is only one aspect of development, and it may be that if there *is* some delay in this area there may be delays in other areas too. There's only one nervous system controlling everything we do, and if it's impaired in some way, other aspects of behaviour might be affected. So don't be surprised if these people seem more interested in other aspects of the child's history – such as how well he plays, when he sat up, or when he learned to walk. Think about the child's general behaviour before you go, so that you have some information available. *Does* he play well? Does he pay attention? Does he seem to understand you? And (if you've noticed that these are all male pronouns), the same questions apply to girls as well.

This first step into the surgery is not an easy one. It's almost like admitting the child is ill. And no one wants to be thought of as an over-anxious parent. But there comes a point when you'll want to know whether there's anything to be concerned about. After all, if the child *isn't* developing language in the normal way, the sooner you know the sooner you can do something about it.

A word of warning. I don't know why it is, but some doctors tend to react to parental anxieties about language in a very superficial way. Perhaps it's because language handicaps don't figure prominently in a doctor's training. Whatever the reason, you may find yourself faced with a doctor who is as unclear about the possible problems as you are. If you don't get asked several questions about the child's background, or if you are too readily given the response 'Don't worry, (s)he'll grow out of it', then you have a right to be suspicious. It's time to move on to the next stage of enquiry.

There are several specialists who will be able to advise. There are paediatricians – doctors who have specialized in the physical growth and development of the whole child. There are psychologists, who study all aspects of children's mental and social development. And above all, there are speech therapists, whose role is to advise on all aspects of emerging language abilities in children, when these seem to be developing abnormally. They can all be contacted through your family doctor, or information about the services in your area can be obtained directly from your local health authority.

If all goes well, you'll be faced with nothing more than a case of late development. But for as many as 2–3 per cent of all pre-school children, things don't work out so well. There may be a genuine 'language delay', a failure of the normal processes of language learning to work to time. These children may not begin to produce clear words until well into their third year, or even later. Once they start to use some language, they progress very slowly, and fall still further behind. They may have difficulties in speaking, or in comprehending your speech, or both. Their problems may affect vocabulary, grammar or pronunciation, or all three. They may be very reluctant to use any language they have acquired. And they may develop ways of speaking which are quite outside the normal patterns – strange sequences of word order, or bizarre meanings for words.

Why children become language handicapped isn't at all clear. In some cases you can put it down to some more fundamental problem, a consequence of some early brain damage, perhaps. A child who is deaf, or partially hearing, will also be likely to show signs of severe language delay. But in the majority of cases there is no obvious medical reason for the failure of language to develop normally. You can have a child who is intelligent, socially aware, sensitive . . . and yet language may not come. In many cases, it's possible to see a link between the poor language and poor ability in other areas of behaviour. In particular, a significant number of language handicapped children also have poor memories and find it difficult to pay attention to what is going on around them. But there is no sign of a single cause which can explain all the language difficulties which affect children.

One thing is clear, if there is *any* sign of this kind of thing taking place, you need to hit it hard, as early as possible. The child needs to be placed in the care of a speech therapist and given regular help. Unfortunately, this is something easier said than done in Britain, in view of the tragic shortage of speech therapists. There are less than 5,000 full-time speech therapists for the whole country at the time of writing, and they have to service the needs of the adult population as well. In the United States, there are about 30,000 speech pathologists – different label, same job – but nor is this generous in view of the much greater population. What this means is that it is very difficult to obtain the degree of intensive help which children with a language problem desperately need if they are to make best use of their time before they go to school. Don't blame the therapist, if all (s)he can offer is half an hour's therapy a week. The blame lies elsewhere, in a system which pays less attention to the health needs of its community than it should.

It's a shame to end on a sour note. But if you've got a language handicapped child, or know one, you'll realize that there are few conditions quite so devastating. Language disability is not a matter of life or death. It's not like cancer or heart disease. Children survive – but to what kind of life? Without the right kind of help at the right time, children can arrive at school socially isolated and linguistically quite unprepared for the demands which will be made upon them. They are trying to cope with the kind of complexity we saw in Chapter 6 using the linguistic resources I was describing in Chapters 2 or 3. They haven't a chance without special help. They will get further and further behind, become more and more isolated, and end up at the bottom of the heap of unemployed. For which employer will take on someone who can't communicate?

So, if you've had an enjoyable, trouble-free period of language acquisition with your child, that's marvellous. This is how it should be and that's why, throughout this book, I've stressed the enjoyment which can be had simply by listening carefully to what children say, and plotting their progress over the years. To study your own child's developing language can be a source of pride and delight. But don't forget to spare a thought for those who find in their child's language a source of anxiety and pain.

"*How can Mummy suddenly start calling you Jennifer after all these years, Button?*"

Appendix 1 | Your child's first fifty words

	Word	Meaning/situation in which it was used	Date first heard
1			
2			
3			
4			
5			
6			
7			
8			
9			
10			
11			
12			
13			
14			
15			
16			
17			
18			
19			
20			
21			
22			

	Word	Meaning/situation in which it was used	Date first heard
23			
24			
25			
26			
27			
28			
29			
30			
31			
32			
33			
34			
35			
36			
37			
38			
39			
40			
41			
42			
43			
44			
45			
46			
47			
48			
49			
50			

Appendix 2 | Your child's sentence length

The way to calculate a child's sentence length is outlined on p. 139. Use pages 226–7 and 228–9 to lay out your data. Leave at least three months between samples, otherwise the results may not be very different.

Name: Age: Recording date:
Recording situation:

Sentences	Word total	Sentences	Word total
1	26		
2	27		
3	28		
4	29		
5	30		
6	31		
7	32		
8	33		
9	34		
10	35		
11	36		
12	37		
13	38		
14	39		
15	40		
16	41		
17	42		
18	43		
19	44		
20	45		
21	46		
22	47		
23	48		
24	49		
25	50		

Sentences	Word total	Sentences	Word total
51		76	
52		77	
53		78	
54		79	
55		80	
56		81	
57		82	
58		83	
59		84	
60		85	
61		86	
62		87	
63		88	
64		89	
65		90	
66		91	
67		92	
68		93	
69		94	
70		95	
71		96	
72		97	
73		98	
74		99	
75		100	

Total Number of Words = _____ ÷ 100 = Mean Sentence Length _____

Name: Age: Recording date:
Recording situation:

Sentences	Word total	Sentences	Word total
1		26	
2		27	
3		28	
4		29	
5		30	
6		31	
7		32	
8		33	
9		34	
10		35	
11		36	
12		37	
13		38	
14		39	
15		40	
16		41	
17		42	
18		43	
19		44	
20		45	
21		46	
22		47	
23		48	
24		49	
25		50	

Sentences	Word total	Sentences	Word total
51		76	
52		77	
53		78	
54		79	
55		80	
56		81	
57		82	
58		83	
59		84	
60		85	
61		86	
62		87	
63		88	
64		89	
65		90	
66		91	
67		92	
68		93	
69		94	
70		95	
71		96	
72		97	
73		98	
74		99	
75		100	

Total Number of Words = _____ ÷ 100 = Mean Sentence Length _____

Appendix 3 | Your child's consonant clusters

Listed below are all the common two-element consonant clusters in English. There isn't space to list all the three-element ones at the end of words (as in *jumps*), but there's room to note the first ones down as they occur. The sounds are written in phonetic symbols, not letters of the alphabet, but an example of each cluster is given in ordinary spelling, so that you'll know which one it is.

Word beginning			In use (√)				In use (√)
bj	as in	*beauty*	☐	ʃr	as in	*shred*	☐
bl		*blow*	☐	sj		*suit*	☐
br		*break*	☐	sk		*score*	☐
dj		*duke*	☐	sl		*slow*	☐
dr		*draw*	☐	sm		*small*	☐
dw		*dwarf*	☐	sn		*snow*	☐
fj		*few*	☐	sp		*spit*	☐
fl		*flow*	☐	st		*stop*	☐
fr		*frog*	☐	sw		*sweet*	☐
gl		*glue*	☐	skr		*screw*	☐
gr		*grow*	☐	skw		*squash*	☐
hj		*huge*	☐	spl		*splash*	☐
kj		*cute*	☐	spr		*spring*	☐
kl		*clear*	☐	str		*string*	☐
kr		*crew*	☐	stj		*stew*	☐
kw		*queen*	☐	tj		*tune*	☐
mj		*music*	☐	tr		*true*	☐
nj		*news*	☐	tw		*twice*	☐
pl		*play*	☐	θr		*three*	☐
pr		*pray*	☐	θw		*thwack*	☐
				vj		*view*	☐

Others

Word ending		In use (√)		In use (√)
bd	as in *rubbed*	☐	nd as in *sand*	☐
bz	*rubs*	☐	ndʒ *range*	☐
dz	*lads*	☐	ns *bounce*	☐
dʒd	*barged*	☐	nt *sent*	☐
fs	*laughs*	☐	nθ *month*	☐
ft	*soft*	☐	nʃ *lunch*	☐
gd	*bagged*	☐	nz *runs*	☐
gz	*bags*	☐	ŋd *hanged*	☐
kt	*act*	☐	ŋk *sink*	☐
lb	*bulb*	☐	ŋz *bangs*	☐
ld	*pulled*	☐	ps *hops*	☐
ldʒ	*bulge*	☐	pt *slept*	☐
lf	*self*	☐	pθ *depth*	☐
lk	*milk*	☐	ʃt *washed*	☐
lm	*film*	☐	sk *ask*	☐
lp	*help*	☐	sp *lisp*	☐
ls	*else*	☐	st *post*	☐
lʃ	*Welsh*	☐	ts *pots*	☐
lt	*melt*	☐	tθ *eighth*	☐
ltʃ	*gulch*	☐	θt *earthed*	☐
lv	*solve*	☐	θs *baths*	☐
lz	*walls*	☐	tʃt *latched*	☐
md	*formed*	☐	ðd *breathed*	☐
mf	*triumph*	☐	ðz *breathes*	☐
mp	*jump*	☐	vd *loved*	☐
mθ	*warmth*	☐	vz *loves*	☐
mz	*comes*	☐	zd *buzzed*	☐

Others

Appendix 4 | Sentences to imitate

You can use these sentences to see how your child's ability to imitate develops. Re-read *Things to do 5* (pp. 172–4) before you start.

Place a tick on the left of each line, if the imitation is perfect. Place it on the right, if the child makes a complete hash of it. And place the tick in the middle, if there are just one or two small inaccuracies in the grammar. Ignore any differences in pronunciation.

	Date 1	Date 2	Date 3	Date 4
1. Hello.				
2. Man.				
3. Jumping.				
4. Green.				
5. Horses.				
6. What?				
7. Man running.				
8. Kick ball.				
9. Look there.				
10. Where girl?				
11. What doing?				
12. Big car.				
13. My house.				
14. In garden.				
15. Sitting down.				
16. See a house.				
17. Go in there.				
18. That boy swimming.				
19. Cat is running.				
20. The dog is sitting.				
21. I saw a dog.				
22. The lady stroked the cat.				
23. The man is reading a book.				
24. The girl is happy.				
25. The cars are ready.				

	Date 1	Date 2	Date 3	Date 4
26. Put the book down.	——	——	——	——
27. Where's the man gone?	——	——	——	——
28. What's the lady doing?	——	——	——	——
29. The bus went into the garage.	——	——	——	——
30. A big red bus and a nice new car.	——	——	——	——
31. He can see a cat and a dog.	——	——	——	——
32. I saw a car today.	——	——	——	——
33. The man went home on a bus.	——	——	——	——
34. The lady is cleaning the floor with a cloth.	——	——	——	——
35. The postman gave the boy a letter.	——	——	——	——
36. I saw a man in a coat.	——	——	——	——
37. I jumped over a big red gate.	——	——	——	——
38. Mary ate an apple and John ate a banana.	——	——	——	——
39. The man walked to town and then he went on the bus.	——	——	——	——
40. The lady laughed when she saw the clown.	——	——	——	——
41. The milkman said that his van was broken.	——	——	——	——
42. After John washed his face, he brushed his teeth.	——	——	——	——
43. When the bus came, the people got on.	——	——	——	——
44. The tiny mouse was chased by a big cat.	——	——	——	——
45. I've read the book that you gave me.	——	——	——	——
46. I saw the boy who gave you the letter.	——	——	——	——
47. The man who was in the shop is eating an apple.	——	——	——	——
48. It was in the garden that I found the ball.	——	——	——	——
49. There were lots of people standing in the street.	——	——	——	——
50. The man went on a bus, the lady went on a train, and the boy went on a boat.	——	——	——	——

Appendix 5 | The things they say: 4 – Your turn

You've seen some of my collection of child language anecdotes in the first three parts of 'The things they say'. You might like to add your own favourite stories to this list, using the following pages.

Appendix 6 | Games which help language

It's difficult to think of a game where language doesn't have some role to play, but some games are particularly good at focusing on certain aspects of spoken language. Here's a selection which can be used with children in the pre-school period.

Large pictures, in full colour, containing a mass of detail, are some of the best materials to get a child talking. Magazine advertisements are often very attractive.

Pre-reading books For example, the Ladybird 'Talkabout' books. They contain many interesting pictures and picture stories, which can provide the focus for a conversation, as well as special tasks which focus on spoken language, such as 'Which noise does each animal make?'.

Favourite toys which involve many components are good for vocabulary development, such as a doll's house and furniture, a farm and animals, or a set of Star Wars implements. Make sure there's a team of toy dolls to be involved in all these places. Incidentally, boys get as much fun out of a doll's house as do girls.

Do what I do. You take turns to instruct each other in a sequence of events, such as 'Touch your nose, clap your hands, scratch your ear'. Good for listening comprehension as well as the production of sentence sequences.

Hunt the . . . anything – bricks, pennies, toy cars . . . Parent and child take turns to hide and find. 'Where's the car? Is it under the chair? Behind the clock? . . .' The game makes use of a lot of spatial language, and is particularly useful if the parent has to stay in one place (e.g. while cooking, feeding another child, and so on).

What am I thinking of? Parent and child take turns to describe an object in a room, one feature at a time. 'It's something big . . . with four legs . . .' The game helps the development of vocabulary by making the child focus on the features of an object which are central to its meaning.

What's the difference? There are lots of puzzle books which show the child two pictures, identical in all but a few respects. The game is to spot the differences, but the child has to say what the differences are at the same time. Good for the development of complex sentences, especially those which make contrasts, comparisons, and so on.

Tell me what you're doing. Share out two sets of toys, so that you and the child have got exactly the same things (bricks, pieces of Lego, etc.). Sit so that you cannot see each other (or put a screen between you). The child has to make something, and then tell you how to place your things to produce the same result. Very good for developing spatial words and sentence sequences.

Put these in order. There are several sets of cards which tell a story if they're placed in the correct order. Deal them out randomly. The child has to sort them out, and then tell the story. Good for sentence sequences. Also, see if the child can tell the story again *without* the pictures.

Pretend games. With any kind of action figures. Parent and child each take a character, and have to act out a scene, using the language which would be appropriate to that character. Helps the development of role play.

Crazy world. Draw a picture of a familiar scene, but put something incongruous into it, such as a car with two steering wheels, or a bicycle with only one wheel. The child has to find what's odd, and say why. If you can't draw, you may be able to find picture books which go in for this kind of thing, especially in children's annuals. Theo LeSieg's *Wacky Wednesday* is a book entirely based on this principle. Develops vocabulary and figurative expression.

Cut-outs which can be assembled in different combinations are good for prompting vocabulary contrasts and sequences of related sentences. The child provides you with a commentary as the cut-outs are assembled. Alternatively, you can keep the cut-outs yourself, and the child has to ask you for them.

Puppets are very useful in getting children to use questions, commands, and other kinds of language which they may not so readily use to adults. A child may not wish to 'command' an adult, but a puppet is different.

What's missing? Show a small selection of familiar objects. Take one away and see if the child can remember which it is. The task helps to train memory in relation to vocabulary. But don't take turns on this one, if you can possibly help it, otherwise you might begin to feel very depressed, when you fail more than the child does.

Appendix 7 | Further reading

There are many books available if you want to take your interest in child language acquisition further. Here is a short selection.

Short introductions

Jerome Bruner, *Child's Talk: Learning to Use Language*, Oxford University Press, 1983.
V. J. Cook, *Young Children and Language*, Edward Arnold, 1979.
Peter and Jill De Villiers, *Early Language*, Fontana, 1979.
Margaret Donaldson, *Children's Minds*, Fontana, 1978.
Catherine Garvey, *Children's Talk*, Fontana, 1984.
Ronald Macaulay, *Generally Speaking: How Children Learn Language*, Newbury House, 1980.
Iona and Peter Opie, *The Lore and Language of Schoolchildren*, Oxford University Press, 1960.
Thelma Weeks, *Born to Talk*, Newbury House, 1979.

More advanced reading

Alan Cruttenden, *Language in Infancy and Childhood*, Manchester University Press/St Martin's Press, 1979.
Jill and Peter De Villiers, *Language Acquisition*, Harvard University Press, 1978.
Paul Fletcher, *A Child's Learning of English*, Blackwell, 1985.
Paul Fletcher and Michael Garman (eds), *Language Acquisition*, Cambridge University Press, 2nd edn, 1985.
Michael McTear, *Children's Conversation*, Blackwell, 1985.

The vast majority of the references to research projects in this book have been taken from the pages of the *Journal of Child Language* (Cambridge University Press), which is the main academic journal in this field. To find the original paper, look up the author's name in the index to vols 1–

10, which is bound into vol. 12.2 (June 1985). Another relevant journal, which is read mainly by teachers, is *Child Language Teaching and Therapy* (published by Edward Arnold).